Word Play

The difference between the almost right word and the right word is really a large matter—it's the difference between the lightning bug and the lightning.

—1888 LETTER FROM MARK TWAIN TO GEORGE BAINTON

Word Play

Building Vocabulary Across Texts and Disciplines, Grades 6–12

Sandra R. Whitaker

HEINEMANN
Portsmouth, NH

Heinemann
361 Hanover Street
Portsmouth, NH 03801–3912
www.heinemann.com

Offices and agents throughout the world

The author and publisher wish to thank those who have generously given permission to reprint borrowed material:

Figure 5.5: "Probable Passage" adapted from *When Kids Can't Read* by Kylene Beers. Copyright © 2003 by Kylene Beers. Published by Heinemann, Portsmouth, NH. All rights reserved.

Library of Congress Cataloging-in-Publication Data
Whitaker, Sandra.
 Word play : building vocabulary across texts and disciplines, grades 6–12 / Sandra R. Whitaker.
     p. cm.
 Includes bibliographical references and index.
 ISBN-13: 978-0-325-01372-5
 ISBN-10: 0-325-01372-1
   1. Vocabulary—Study and teaching. 2. Language arts. I. Title.
 LB1574.5.W45 2008
 372.44—dc22   2007043906

Editor: Harvey Daniels
Production: Elizabeth Valway
Cover design: Bernadette Skok
Composition: Cape Cod Compositors
Manufacturing: Louise Richardson

Printed in the United States of America on acid-free paper
12 11 10 09 08   RRD   1 2 3 4 5

This book is dedicated to

My grandmothers, Lois Pineau Brewick and
Edith Salome Hemphill Anderson,
who deeply loved words and taught me to do the same

And to the Glory of God, who gave us the gift of language

Contents

Foreword

I double majored in college—English and German—and was generally the exception to the trend in class preferences. My English major peers stood in line (it was a few decades before computers took over university registration) to get in the choice literature classes. How amazing, they noted, that a student could get credit for reading and thinking about novels, poems, and plays!

In pursuit of a degree, I read my share of great and not-so-great books, of course, but the registration lines I gravitated toward were the ones that gave me entry into courses on the history of the English language, etymology, and vocabulary. My registration lines were shorter, of course, but the classes they represented were endlessly fascinating to me. There was an actual history behind how the verb *to be* came to be populated by unlikely cousins such as *am*, *were*, *been*, and *is*. There was a quilt of ancestry hanging just about the food we eat—French, German, Persian, Greek, British, Indian, Aboriginal, Chinese. The myths I'd read with less than total relish in junior high had left the anthologies and migrated into the sciences and poetry. Words captured the essence of people they came to memorialize. They had the seed of humor just beneath their surface.

I'm not sure I understood then—or even now—why I was so captivated by the intricacies of the language into which I was born. I think some of the fascination was that words showed me connections among subjects and ideas that had previously remained disconnected in my thinking. Some of the satisfaction came from encountering a whole new way to make sense of the world around me and beyond. It was also empowering to begin to understand the language I'd learned to speak unconsciously. Previously, I'd been like a driver who gets around quite adequately in a car but has no idea what to do when the vehicle breaks down. The study of words gave me the capacity to name the parts of the "vehicle" that transported me, to grasp their function, and to take a stab at modifying them when the need arose.

It's no surprise, then, that when I became an English teacher, my students were victims of my fascination with language. We played with words, dissected them, learned their genealogy, called on their humor, were transported to other times and places in their service, saw our own histories and personalities reflected in them. Stories were good. Words were better.

It never made sense to me to ask students to memorize lists of words. That would have been like asking them to memorize the phone book instead of learning about the people in town. Instead, we wallowed in words. We did choral reading and poems for multiple voices as a way to hear words. We created word play. We learned about root words and searched for derivatives. We looked at ways words are created—and created words for things, moments, emotions we had all experienced but which were unnamed in our language. We looked at words in other languages that have no counterparts in English. We took photos of weird words in the world around us and corrected spelling and grammar on signs. We learned the International Phonetic Alphabet as a new way to become sensitive to sounds. We looked at aphorisms across times and places to understand how they reflected the cultures that spawned them. We studied how names have evolved over time. We "adopted" and studied languages we'd never heard of, and we learned how people go into cultures with disappearing languages to record and preserve them. We puzzled over words in stories, using clues to unlock their meaning or speculating on why an author might have chosen a particular word when so many synonyms were possible.

I was pretty good at helping students understand how language mirrors its culture and tells the story of human beings—including how their own language both shaped and was shaped by the kids themselves. I like to think the work we did was a catalyst for the evolution of a fair number of language connoisseurs and even a few language junkies.

When I read the manuscript for *Word Play*, however, I had the response I always have when I read a really high quality book about teaching. It made me want to relive my two decades of classroom teaching. I could have done a much better job of empowering my students with language had I had this book as a young teacher.

Sandra Whitaker does several things in the book that seem very important to me. First, she resists the inclination to provide teachers with a "bag of tricks" that is rooted in nothing more than the desire to have something to do Monday morning. Understandable as that desire is, it doesn't help us grow deep roots in the disciplines we teach. This book provides practical strategies for increasing students' power with and power over language, but always nests those strategies in an understanding of their origins and why they matter for learners. Second, the book consistently provides a context for the strategies it commends. Classroom scenarios and student examples help us see how the ideas play out in the classroom. Third, the author doesn't assume that good strategies are good for all students in the same way at the same time, and so the book makes clear ways in which the instructional approaches can be used differently to benefit different students. Fourth, the book places vocabulary instruction as a central and feasible element key to effective teaching in all disciplines. The book teaches teachers first and then teaches us how to teach our students better.

It is the confluence of Sandra's own long, rich, and reflective experience as a learner, an English teacher, and a supervisor of language arts that makes the book possible. The book, in turn, makes it possible for teachers in all subjects to help their students become competent, confident readers and self-aware thinkers through the power of words.

Carol Ann Tomlinson
University of Virginia

Acknowledgments

ny writing project ought to be a collaborative effort. Even when a writer is locked in her own office and hammering away on the keyboard, the reader is ever present. In the most joyful way, writing *is* a collaborative process. And writing a book is *most definitely* a collaborative effort. For that, I am most grateful.

Without Harvey "Smokey" Daniels, Zoe Ryder, Lisa Luedeke, and the amazingly talented and empathetic folks at Heinemann, this book would not have happened. At times, I rued the moment I spoke up in one of Smokey's workshops that led to this book, but you all kept me on track—pointing the way, offering assistance, and cheerleading as necessary. Your contributions make this text richer and made the experience wonderful.

Each day I am honored to work with truly inspiring and dedicated teachers in Albemarle County Public Schools. In many ways, this book lends a voice to our shared journey. I particularly wish to thank those teachers who allowed me to team teach and who helped me to collect student samples: Pat Harder, Chad Sansing, Natalie Wood, Victoria Megginson, Natasha Heny, Cathy Glover, Lewis "Cubby" Fox, and Patty Parmiter.

The road to high-powered vocabulary instruction was often rocky and filled with unexpected stumbling blocks. I am fortunate to have had amazing mentors along the way: Carol Hawkins, Ann Richardson, Anne Cunningham, Doc Larrick, Jane Hansen, and Carol Tomlinson.

I am particularly appreciative of the insights Dr. Rollin David Larrick (Doc) shared during our interview together in May 2007. I've never met another soul who knows as much about language (after all, he reads all of the Germanic and Romance medieval languages) or who is brave enough to do the *New York Times* Sunday crossword puzzle in pen! I am proud to be one of your unofficial students.

Over the years, I have been fortunate to work with my mom, Ruth Larson, in many different veins of education, this project included. Her pinch-hitting with student samples and her incomparable encouragement made the last few weeks of pulling everything together possible.

Always, kids are at the heart of the work. Although their names are changed in the text, many students did *extra work over the summer* to help get this title into production. To Elizabeth, Kristen, Aubrey, Conner, Irma, Gabby, Stevie, Katherine, Hannah, Taylor, Alexus, Chenaya, Maggie, Hillary, Alex, Samantha, Rebecca, Josie, and Catherine, my many, many thanks.

My heartfelt appreciation goes to all of those on the sidelines who both coach me and cheer me on, pushing me toward new personal goals. Don Vale and Pat Hughes, who checked in regularly—and at times, daily—to make sure I was still writing. Carrie Neeley, Cyndi Wells, Courtney Stewart, Sujatha Hampton, and Kristen Williams, the best literacy team ever—anywhere. Carol Clark, friend extraordinaire, who keeps me laughing. Sara Kajder, who was always a phone call away (so, so good to have you back in Virginia!). Jennifer Jones, who helps me keep the demands of my life in perspective and in balance. Ruth Larson and Dave Brewick, my parents, who are my most important teachers and biggest fans.

Finally, because this is the acknowledgments section, I should acknowledge that living with a high-maintenance and sometimes neurotic overachiever can't be easy, and my husband (Jeff), kids (Josie and Michael), and dogs (Aspen and Steamboat) put up with me daily. As I write, my husband is making dinner while supervising a third grader's homework and simultaneously ensuring that the three-year-old doesn't color on the walls, jump on the furniture, or hurt the dogs. And the nine-year-old is doing her homework without a battle. And the three-year-old is "helping" and "staying out of Mom's way." Bless you all. Not only do you support my work, you support me. The daily blessing of you in my life makes the journey beautiful.

Introduction

The students from my first few years as a high school English teacher would probably laugh to see my name on the cover of a book about effective vocabulary instruction. Like most educators, I've tried some techniques I'd rather forget. In fact, I've worked to mentally block out my first year in the classroom. But as all teachers know, those early slipups become our own best teachers.

The principal of my first school required every teacher to assign ten vocabulary words each week. We had a rotating schedule on which we tested these words so that students wouldn't have seven vocabulary tests in one day. Every teacher in the building, including me, followed this practice. I don't believe that principal had any malicious intent. In fact, he instituted the expectation because of gaps he saw in his own child's learning. As the instructional leader in the building, he was attempting to address concerns about the kids' educational experiences—and, sixteen years ago, he didn't have a wealth of research to guide him.

Instead of questioning the principal's practice, I adopted it. This was my first teaching job, and I didn't want to break the rules. Plus, I knew that requiring students to learn words wouldn't harm them. So for a while I followed my colleagues' lead, taking the difficult words from a text we were studying and assigning them as vocabulary words. Unfortunately, I had no way of knowing whether I was selecting the "right" words or even words that my students didn't already know. Many of the words I chose had little relevance beyond the text at hand, and students quickly forgot them.

My next idea was to use the most frequent words on the SAT. Because I worked primarily with sophomores and juniors in those early years, it seemed logical that knowing the words for such a high-stakes assessment would benefit them. I even made flashcards, which I still have, for the 500 most frequent SAT vocabulary words. During those few minutes after a fire drill had hijacked a lesson, the only time I could find to revisit previously "learned" words, I would grab the index card box, and together we would review the words that had been assigned earlier in the year. Again, I knew I wasn't hurting the kids, but I could see that the information wasn't transferring into their writing or deepening their understanding of language structures.

At the recommendation of my language arts curriculum coordinator, I even had groups of students act out words, to make them more tactile. This came at a time when teachers in our school system were expected to triple-code lesson plans for Howard Gardner's Multiple Intelligences. I still shake my head when I think of my former students acting out random vocabulary words because I hadn't been able to code "kinesthetic" on enough lesson plans.

If the goal was for students to own a lot of words, none of the practices I had tried was working. I may have been meeting the school system's expectations, but I wasn't meeting my students' needs. So, as I gained confidence in teaching, I began to experiment.

An egregious speller myself, I understood that people know and use more words than they can spell. For example, just yesterday my three-year-old sang me his "EBCs." His understanding of letters is just forming, and he has no concept of spelling. Still, he speaks in complete sentences and knows a couple thousand words. So while I understand that spelling is a necessary skill, I also knew it wasn't the key to vocabulary development.

For my students, I started to group words conceptually. While I still tested spelling to meet the principal's expectations, I focused more on making sure that students understood how the words related and how to use them in speech and in writing. This practice led me to the academic vocabulary necessary for students to understand the disciplines of language and literature, but it also took away from the focus on words in context.

I toyed with the idea of assigning twenty words—ten academic and ten from the reading—but I knew students would rat me out, not wanting to do double spelling work for my class. Why I was afraid of that, I don't know. So instead of assigning more words, I looked for ways to embed vocabulary instruction into different aspects of our daily work.

Soon I had developed a variety of methods for front-loading vocabulary, teaching students key words that would appear in a text we were studying before reading the text. I quit focusing on words that make meaning for only a few texts and instead focused on words that make meaning across texts and across disciplines. The words that make up 95 percent of all text are words that most kids already know. Instead of those words, I focused on the conceptual meaning makers, the other 5 percent, which are the words that carry the most meaning for a particular text—either through specific language or for underlying meaning. I stopped thinking that every word students will need to understand a text actually appears in the text; instead, I started thinking about the background knowledge students would need as they encounter a text.

At this point, students in my class were receiving solid vocabulary instruction in two areas: academic vocabulary and words in context. I could see the transfer into their writing starting to happen, but too slowly. And what about those SAT words? If I wanted students to understand how words relate to other words, I knew I needed to address the *structures* of language, but I didn't know how. I had taken a linguistics course in college, but that hardly seemed enough. Sure, I taught my students prefixes and suffixes, but the process wasn't exactly loads of fun. If my students retained the information, they did so not because of my wonderful teaching but because some affixes (the umbrella under which prefixes and suffixes fit) appear so frequently in our language that it would be hard *not* to know them.

It was in my students' writing that the gap in my instruction showed most clearly. Students were raiding the thesaurus without any sense of the nuances of words, making random choices that rendered some of their essays nearly incomprehensible. One student wrote: I am infatuated with chocolate. While the sentence works technically, the context is wrong. I knew I needed to ramp up my own abilities with the structure of language if I wanted to help my students.

I took some classes to refresh my linguistics knowledge. Digging into my brain for the Spanish and French I used to speak, I found I knew a lot about the influx of words from other cultures and languages. I became more interested in the etymology of English, and I began to share that enthusiasm with my students, often asking, "What do you think might be the story behind that word?"

Together, my students and I transformed vocabulary instruction into something meaningful. The journey spanned ten years, three schools, and more than a thousand students. I stumbled many times as I experimented with lessons, methods, and ideas to help children learn language. In the end, I found that the solution is as simple, and as complex, as teaching children to play with words.

Why This Book Now?

Through ten years of experimentation, I've learned a great deal. Of them, the most important is this: You don't have to resort to linguistics courses or immersion in other languages to change the way you teach vocabulary. And you don't have to become an academic researcher in this area; I certainly haven't. I am a teacher who has struggled to meet students' diverse, ever-changing needs. I have taught, on average, 150 students each year in middle and high school classrooms. I have read widely, putting suggested strategies into practice and then modifying them for my students. I have relied on the research of others, the experts and explorers on vocabulary development whose studies have illuminated us over the past couple of decades.

Children who are immersed in language-rich environments develop rich vocabularies (Beck, McKeown, and Kucan 2002). When children are exposed to high-powered vocabulary in their daily lives, and when they are encouraged to ask questions about how words work, the process of acquiring new words becomes play. Children begin to own and use not only a high volume of words but also those word structures that are the foundation of English.

Many teachers do not explicitly teach vocabulary development, hoping that through the reading process alone, children will acquire enough words to access the demands of various disciplines. Research indicates that such an instructional approach leaves much to chance (Biemiller 1999, 2001; Nagy and Anderson 1984; Cunningham and Stanovich 2003). The most effective vocabulary instruction teaches directly those roots and words that will have the greatest impact on a child's understanding of language structures (Biemiller 2001; Beck, McKeown, and Kucan 2002; Estes and Larrick 2007; Ganske 2000; Marzano and Pickering 2005).

In addition, research indicates that after decoding skills are partialed out (or separated from the other components of reading), vocabulary development has a significant impact on fluent reading (Cunningham and Stanovich 2003), and between a .75 and .8 correlation with reading comprehension (Cunningham 2004). That's significant! Reading is a reciprocal process—the very act of reading increases a child's vocabulary—but the vocabulary a child brings to the reading process also greatly impacts fluency and comprehension. In addition to providing children with lots of time to simply read, comprehension and fluency will be greatly enhanced when teachers also provide students with strategies that they can use independently to tackle unknown words when they are heard or read.

Typically, children are taught three basic strategies to use when they encounter unknown words: "skip (or substitute) and read on," "sound it out," and "use context." While these are useful strategies, a student must know when (and how) to employ each if they are to be used effectively. For example, the "skip and read on" strategy works well if the unknown word is a proper noun.

Martin is reading a novel set in Paris. He has encountered the name *Mme. Chouinard*, and he is stuck. Afraid that if he skips over the confusing term he will not understand the story, he asks his teacher for help. She explains that he can either skip the name altogether, or he can substitute a feminine pronoun or a known name (Jill) as a marker and still make meaning of the passage. She continues to explain that as long as Martin continues to distinguish this individual's name from other names in the passage, the specific name is not necessary. Breathing a sigh of relief, Martin chooses *Lucy* and continues reading.

The "sound it out" strategy helps the reader only if (1) he has sufficient understanding of a variety of language patterns [c/v/c (consonant/vowel/consonant) will produce a short vowel, silent *e* produces a long vowel, etc.], and (2) the word is one he has heard and understands but hasn't read frequently enough for it to become a sight word.

> Chase encounters *gridiron* and pauses. He's unsure of the word but knows to attempt sounding it out. His first attempt produces grid-iron, and he recognizes the term from football. Satisfied that this is correct, he continues reading. Kelly also pauses at *gridiron*, sounds it out effectively, and relies on her background in theater to check the pronunciation. Justin, however, is stuck. Encountering the same word and using the same strategy, Justin produces gri-dir-on. It makes no sense. Not knowing another strategy, Justin continues reading, becoming more and more confused and frustrated as the word continues to appear.

"Using context" may allow a student to distinguish between multiple meanings and may also aid in the "sound it out" strategy. But used alone, because of the complexity of word nuances, context often doesn't provide enough information for a reader to make meaning of a completely unknown word. In addition, the farther the context clues are from the unknown word, the less likely a student is to determine its meaning.

These three strategies, while good to keep in mind, don't provide children with all they need to know to develop strong vocabulary skills. Because they specifically address receptive vocabulary, they are best used while reading or listening. Equally (perhaps even more) important is *productive* vocabulary—the words we produce to communicate our own ideas. Without transfer of new vocabulary into speech and writing, can we really say a student owns words?

As a high school student myself, I participated in an exchange program to France. I quickly became aware that the receptive language I had "learned" in American classrooms was not much help in my attempts to produce that language to communicate my thoughts. In order to truly communicate, my vocabulary had to extend beyond the basics—way beyond! While I could understand most of what my host family said (Thank goodness I understood when my French host mother asked if I would like liver for supper!), initially I couldn't produce enough language to join in the conversation. I was trapped in my own head! Even the family dog tilted his head, as if understanding that my French wasn't up to snuff, when I opened my mouth to ask a simple question. Explicitly teaching strategies for developing not only receptive vocabulary but productive vocabulary as well can help our students escape that trap.

This book will show you the result of everything I have learned from the research, tried and adapted in my own teaching, and fleshed out with my colleagues. The result: strategies that work with real students in real classrooms. As secondary language arts curriculum coordinator in Albemarle County, Virginia, I help to support more than 1,200 teachers across twenty-six buildings and work directly with teachers in five middle schools and four high schools. When I started this job, students taking the state assessment tests consistently missed questions related to vocabulary; the problem was particularly acute at the middle school level. Understanding that language is the key to learning, I wanted to work with teachers and experts around the nation to find new ways to think about vocabulary instruction. We did, and the changes have made a huge difference.

When I walked through schools four years ago, I may have seen half a dozen word walls (Chapters 2 and 8) in our middle school language arts classrooms. Now I would be hard-pressed to find half a dozen classrooms without them. When I score portfolios, I see that more and more teachers have used strategies like morpheme manipulatives (Chapter 2) to activate students' prior knowledge and to introduce new morphemes (the smallest portion of a word that carries meaning). I see evidence of effective vocabulary instruction daily.

Earlier this year, I received an email from a science teacher thanking me for our intense focus on vocabulary instruction in language arts. Because his students were better prepared to grapple with language, he said, he could do a better job of teaching the vocabulary they needed for science. And students tell me that they enjoy reading because their word strategies help them not only to comprehend text but also to read more fluently.

And, yes, our state test scores have improved. Not only do students achieve better scores on the vocabulary-specific questions but overall scores in reading and writing have also increased. Clearly this pleases teachers, administrators, and parents alike. Most important, when I am in classrooms, I see students excited to play with words.

How This Book Is Organized

In this book you'll find three sections that examine the three essential aspects of vocabulary instruction: morphemic structure, conceptual meaning makers, and academic vocabulary. Each section addresses the theoretical—"here's *why* we should teach this"—and then moves to the practical—the strategies for *how* to teach in that area. The numerous student samples show you not only how to set up and use the strategies but also how kids have responded. The strategies are not one-shot lessons but rather tools you can employ throughout the year, and over the years to come. In these pages you'll find none of the infamous vocabulary worksheets, used once and forever forgotten. Instead, you'll find tools that, as they become common practice in your classroom, will deepen students' understanding of language.

To succeed, students need all three aspects of vocabulary instruction. The first, understanding the morphemic structure of words in English, goes beyond simply learning affixes (attachments to the roots of words). Fully understanding language also means learning something about etymology, how words have changed over time, so that students can appreciate the factors that make language dynamic. Because of the Norman invasion, English is a dual language; it's hard to understand the structure we see today without understanding that duality.

The second area of vocabulary instruction, conceptual meaning makers, focuses on the words that constitute only 5 percent of a text yet are essential to understanding. Take the word *papoose*, for example. It's fun to say, and it might help kids clarify an image in reading a story on Native Americans. Aside from that story, however, the word probably doesn't carry much conceptual information. So if the teacher shows numerous pictures of papooses and has students draw and label their own pictures, she's using precious class time on a less-than-crucial point. Instead, the teacher could easily make this word a marker by quickly telling children that a papoose is a young child born to American Indian parents, and asking them simply to substitute *child* for *papoose* as they read. Done.

The final area of vocabulary instruction is academic vocabulary, which includes both words that carry their meaning across disciplines and words that are discipline-specific. For example, the word *analyze* carries its meaning: In science, math, history, and language arts, it means to determine the nature and relationship of the parts of something. On the other hand, the word *bat* has different meanings in different contexts. While those meanings may be related, and we would want to help children to see that relationship, a child who wants to appreciate "Casey at the Bat" will first need to figure out whether the title refers to sports or mammals. Academic vocabulary instruction helps students determine meaning in relation to the discipline being studied, using precise language to communicate complex ideas.

Instruction in all three vocabulary areas—morphemic structure, conceptual meaning makers, and academic vocabulary—allows children to succeed, to understand the underlying structure of language, and to gain the words necessary to access the next grade's content. Without thorough vocabulary instruction, the Matthew Effect (Cunningham and Stanovich 2003) takes hold: The rich (the children who understand language) get richer, and the poor (the children who don't) get poorer. We can never eliminate gaps in achievement until we wipe out this syndrome at the source.

Most of all, children need thorough, lively vocabulary instruction to learn the sheer joy of language. Providing a firm, strong foundation frees students for the adventure of hunting for a word, the delight of selecting just the right one, the pleasure of feeling like an authority, in complete command of language.

How to Use This Book

When visiting a new place full of adventure, I want to do everything rather than exploring more deeply and savoring just a few experiences. As an educator, I encounter the same temptation when approaching a new and helpful resource. I want to try it all, right away. Sometimes I jump in too fast and forget to bring my students along.

As you explore the three sections of this book, I hope you'll do something counterintuitive: Read the theoretical portions first. Yes, your time is limited, and you'd love to jump in and start trying strategies tomorrow. But benefit from my hard-won experience and believe: Understanding the *why* will help you with the *how*. After you've read the theory, take stock of your own teaching practices. What do you already do that works, and what doesn't work so well? Reviewing your practices will help you decide which strategies from the book you might want to experiment with first.

Chose a focus area. Read the strategies for that focus area and try them in your classroom. Seek to make two or three strategies regular features in your instruction, and help students to maximize their benefit. If you and your students master three effective strategies per quarter and use them regularly, by the end of the year you will have significantly improved vocabulary instruction in your classroom.

For example, my students completed an "8-Count" (Chapter 4) as a part of their revision process for every major piece of writing that they took through the writing process. By the end of the first semester, this strategy flew on autopilot in my classroom. I didn't have to remind students; the 8-Count had become part of the culture of our class. That kind of synthesis can't happen if you try too many changes too fast.

Take time for the conversations that will present themselves, and allow yourself time to fail. When things don't go smoothly right away, you'll be tempted to retreat to ineffective strategies that are easy. Resist the temptation and keep pushing for change. Learn with your students. When you feel you've mastered a couple of the strategies, add a few more.

Your instruction will keep evolving not only as your ideas change but as the language itself evolves. Go back fifty years and you have but one mouse, a plain little creature that scurries across the floor and likes cheese. Today, I use the mouse next to my keyboard to scurry around the computer screen. It is plain—black and silver—but I doubt it eats cheese. A preschool-aged child can articulate the difference between those two mice, thus demonstrating an understanding of the evolution of language.

Allow the evolution. Celebrate the understanding. Savor the words!

SECTION ONE

Word Structures

Understanding: Children must play with words.

One sunny afternoon, little Juliet was dancing around on the driveway in front of her house. Meanwhile, her older brother was trying to ride his bike on that same driveway, and little Juliet kept dancing into his path. At first he tried to avoid her but soon became more and more frustrated with the effort. Finally, he looked at his mother and demanded, "Could you please tell her to stop circumbobulating!"

"What a fantastic word!" she exclaimed, smiling in delight at her son's understanding of the morphemic structure of language. "Tell me what *circumbobulating* means."

"Well, she's bouncing up and down and she's moving around in all these circles, and I was thinking that circumbobulating has both of those parts."

"Excellent thinking!"

Why and How to Teach Morphemic Structure

2

Some undereducated adults may have chided the poor boy from the vignette, insisting that *circumbobulating* isn't a word. Isn't it? It may not reside in the dictionary—yet—but it most certainly carries meaning. *Circulus*—or circle—means small ring. One may connect this with *circus* or *circular* or *circumference* or *circumvent*. As a noun, *bob* is a short, jerking motion. The suffix *ate* means to make, and the *ing* suffix is one that is attached to verbs to indicate action. So *circumbobulating* is to make short, jerking motions in a circular fashion. Brilliant!

When we examine morphemic structure closely, it becomes clear that *all* words are made up of these little units of meaning. Children often delight in making up new words by stringing together familiar morphemes. This is creativity in action. In fact, my two youngest brothers, who are significantly younger than the other kids in our family, had their own language. They called each other Bert and Ernie (after the *Sesame Street* characters) and communicated in words that only they fully understood. I marveled at their play interactions—passing and sharing toys, moving on to a different activity, deciding to break for a snack or lunch—all communicated through words only they understood. Children also make up words that relate to proper English. Just the other day, my three-year-old shrieked, "She hitted me!" referring to his older sister. He demonstrated an understanding of regular past tense in English. He will eventually internalize the irregular past tense as his command of language increases, but his temporary use of the word *hitted* uncovers an amazing thought process. This very young child has a conceptual understanding of morphemes. The *ed means* something; it indicates past tense. Most adult native speakers are able to intuit and use morphemic structure correctly in conversation, but often we are doing this without a conscious understanding of how morphemic structure works.

Why Morphemic Structure Matters

Understanding morphemic structure unlocks the language's code and gives individuals access to innumerable words. Sixty-five percent of words in English are constructed from Latin and Greek bases; in fact, several hundred thousand words are built from merely a few hundred morphemes, or meaningful parts (Gunter, Estes, and Mintz 2006). Learning just a few hundred roots actually opens up more than 250,000 words! For this reason, there is considerable power in teaching roots and affixes to our students. Think of those 4,000 words children must learn just to handle what the next grade has to offer, and the 88,700 word families appearing in texts children will encounter up to twelfth grade (Nagy and Anderson 1984).

English is complex. And teaching its structures is a complex process. At its inception, English was primarily an Anglo-Saxon language. After the Norman invasion, English absorbed the Latin of the conquerors to become a dual language, with words having both Anglo-Saxon and Latinate counterparts. Dr. Rollin David Larrick (teacher, linguist, and founder of the innovative vocabulary program Dynamic Literacy) clarifies during an interview, "The Norman invasion made English a bilingual language by nature. The winning side, the Normans, insisted that their language, which was Latinate, be the official language. It was used for all government business and academics—even trade. They forbade the use of Anglo-Saxon language. But the people found ways to preserve their language, speaking it in homes and teaching it to their children—even though it wasn't spoken in public. After approximately fifty years, the two languages melded, although the winning language is still the basis of all academics, government, science, and so on. So every word in English has duality. If you give me a word— either Latinate or Anglo-Saxon, I can give you its counterpart. For example, *cook* and *chef*, *talk* and *converse*, *go away* and *retreat*."

Interesting enough, children still generally learn the Anglo-Saxon words first because they tend to be monosyllabic and have more generalized uses than their Latinate counterparts. Moats (2004) gives this example: *House*, according to *The Oxford English Dictionary*, 2nd Edition, carries nineteen definitions; *habitat*, the Latinate counterpart, carries only two definitions. *House* can be used to describe a personal residence, a tenant dwelling, a theater house, a so on. Why? *House* at its root means dwelling or shelter. *Habitat*, on the other hand, is derived from *habit*, which morphologically

STEP INTO A CLASSROOM

Earlier this year, I visited a middle school classroom where students worked in small groups to generate words around a couple of roots using numerous affixes. I asked the students in one group what they were working on, and this conversation followed:

"Our root words," one red-headed boy replied.

"Okay, what does that mean?" I prodded.

"It means we think of words with this root, here," he answered, pointing to his paper, and indicating *morph/morpho*.

"What does a root do for a word?" I questioned.

Rolling his eyes and likely thinking I must be the dumbest language arts coordinator on the planet, he humored me with, "The root gives the word its meaning."

"Cool," I said, trying to redeem some dignity. "But all of the words on your list are different. Do they really mean the same thing?"

A boy wearing braces jumped in, "No, they have affixes around them, and the affixes change the word just a little bit."

"The prefixes come before the root and the suffixes come after the root," a blonde-haired girl added.

"That's pretty cool," I say.

"No. You know what's *really* cool?" asked the only student in the group who hadn't yet spoken. Due to this boy's rather blank expression through the rest of the conversation, I was surprised that he jumped into the conversation.

"No, honey, what?"

"*All* words work that way."

I honestly couldn't control the smile that crept across my face. As I left the room, I thought to myself, yes, honey, *all* words work that way. A child who so delights in his understanding of words clearly commands power over language and language structures!

means to hold or possess. So a *habitat* relates directly to the being that dwells there.

This duality enriches our language, but it does complicate matters for students (and their teachers!). Children may learn the basic words necessary to communicate their needs and to identify most people, places, things, and actions without learning the more sophisticated (and more specific) Latinate words in English. Because all academic subjects depend on Latinate words for thorough understanding, children benefit in many ways from developing a process for tackling those words when they are encountered.

Learning about morphemic structure gives students another set of strategies to use when reading—beyond "skip and read on," "sound it out," and "use context." Understanding morphemic structure allows students to properly decode and make meaning of multisyllabic words (primarily Latinate), which is particularly useful when those words are decontextualized. Consider the sentence, "It was predestined." In the absence of contextual information, a reader unfamiliar with the word *predestined* is stuck. Without any process for breaking down *predestined*, the reader will not understand the sentence and may not understand the entire passage at hand. However, if the reader knows that *pre* means *before*, and also knows that *destiny* means something that is made firm by fate, he may approximate that something *predestined* was made firm before it happened—or, fated to happen.

Dual Language Examples

Anglo-Saxon	Latinate
food	cuisine
leaf	foliage
car	automobile
mark	signature
desk	bureau
fish tank	aquarium
cross	traverse
stay	remain
change	amend
house	habitat, residence
box	container

From Why to How

Teaching students how to break down words and approximate meaning even when context clues aren't available or helpful provides a tool that gives children a stronger command over unfamiliar words they encounter. Because many of us were not taught to break down words in this way ourselves, it is easy to shy away from teaching morphology. But, teachers, take heart! You don't have to be a linguist to teach morphemic structure well! You must simply be willing to learn to play with the construction and deconstruction of words alongside your students—to ask, when a word like *deconstruction* is encountered, not just, "*What* does that mean?" but "*How* does that mean?"

In addition to simply allowing ourselves to be curious and excited about words, solid vocabulary instruction depends on carving out time to thoughtfully teach our students about morphemic structure. When we plan out which roots, affixes, and combining forms we'll teach our students throughout the year, we ensure that they will have access to appropriate and helpful information as they move through the curriculum. If we assume that students will encounter and understand all of the morphemes appropriate to their level just in the course of their reading, we are missing out on some wonderful opportunities for enhancing their vocabulary development and their curiosity about and ownership of language.

A Quick Review

Some scholars spend entire lifetimes immersed in the study of words. Many excellent books and programs are available on linguistics if you are interested in pursuing your own studies. (The most thorough that I have attended is the LETRS training offered through Sopris West, and I have listed many excellent print resources in the references.) That said, a basic understanding of just a few components of our language will go a long way as you begin working with morphemic structure in your classroom.

Phonemes, Morphemes, and Graphemes (Oh, My!)

Phonemes (from Greek *phon(e)* meaning *sound*) are single, distinctive sounds in speech. We combine phonemes to make words. Morphemes (from Greek *morph* meaning *change*) are the smallest units of meaning in a language. Therefore, morphemes can be anything from an apostrophe to a root. Graphemes (from Greek *graph* meaning *write*) are letters or letter combinations that map, or correspond, to phonemes. English has fewer letters (26) than speech sounds (42), so many graphemes are letter combinations (for example, *ch*).

Affix Basics

Fix comes from Latin (*figere*) and means to *fasten*. So, affixes are morphemes that are "fastened" to roots and modify their meanings. Prefixes (*pre* meaning *before*) come before the root. Examples include *anti* and *sub*. Some prefixes are assimilated, or absorbed, into the initial consonant of the root. For example, the prefix *in* gets assimilated when combined with *regular*, making the word *irregular*. Suffixes (*suf* meaning *upon*) come after the root. Some suffixes are inflectional (*'s*) and others are derivational (*naut*).

Inflections vs. Derivations

By definition, inflection means "the act or result of bending or curving." Keeping that in mind, inflections *bend* words without changing their overall meaning. Inflections are those suffixes that change the form of a word in terms of case, gender, number, tense, person, mood, or voice. For example, *boy* becomes *boys* when the inflection *s* is added.

Derivation, by definition, means "the formation of a word from another word or base." In this way, derivations *change* the word's meaning. Astronaut and astrological become very different words with the addition of the derivations *naut* and *log-ic-al*.

Roots vs. Combining Forms

The bases for Latinate words are called *roots*. The root is the portion of a word that provides its overall meaning. Affixes and combining forms are *added onto* roots to create new words. Combining forms come to us from

Greek. Unlike the Latin roots, which generally appear centrally in a word, Greek combining forms may appear in various parts of a word and are combined with other combining forms or free words. Some combining forms act like prefixes—*hydro*, *photo*, *tele*—while others act like suffixes—*ology*, *logue*. Examples of words containing combining forms include *photograph* and *biology*.

The Seemingly Random *O*

In many cases, word spellings and pronunciations aren't the direct result of stringing morphemes together. The word *synonym* is an example. The combining forms used here are *syn* meaning *together* or *same* and *nym* meaning *name* or *called*. But try saying "synnym!" Technically, that's how the morphemes would be combined, and in writing, it works fine. But language is intended to be spoken, and saying "synnym" out loud tangles the tongue. Insert an *o* and the result is *synonym*. Much easier! Often words that include or are made up entirely of Greek combining forms will include a seemingly random *o*. Often this *o* carries no meaning of its own and was inserted so words could be more easily pronounced.

Strategies Matter

When it comes to teaching morphemic structure, I've learned that strategy matters. When word study isn't playful, it becomes dry quickly, and students lose interest. But when we afford kids opportunities to both study new morphemes and draw on prior knowledge through previously learned words, they start to make connections among words and deepen their understanding of word structures. That said, let's move on to some high-powered and fun activities that engage students in work with morphemes.

Morpheme Manipulatives

Morpheme manipulatives can take many forms. Whether note cards or puzzle pieces or play-dough, teacher-created or student-created, the idea is to encourage children to play with words. Manipulatives allow physical manipulation of word parts, affording students opportunities to move pieces around to make new words and to see connections between words that they might otherwise miss.

Setup

Morpheme manipulatives are cards with morphemes written or printed on them, which can be put together by students to form words. They should be color-coded to maximize student understanding of word parts. (I use yellow for prefixes, blue for roots, and pink for suffixes.) Sticky notes, note cards, and many other items are easily purchased in yellow, blue, and pink, so using those colors allows for many different types of manipulatives to be used interchangeably. These colors are also readily available in highlighters, so students can color-code highlighted morphemes on their papers as well.

Students can make their own manipulatives—this minimizes teacher setup time but does require class or homework time. Teachers may instead opt to create some stock manipulatives that can be used multiple times over several years.

Before creating your manipulatives, it is important to identify relevant morphemes to be studied. Students who are still learning the basic structures of English will benefit most from working with inflections such as *s*, *es*, *ed*, and *ing*. These morphemes help students with the regular structures for nouns and verbs. Later, teachers may add *ly*, *y*, *er*, *est*, *'s*, and *s'* to begin working with adverbs, adjectives, and possessives. The roots used in these situations should be common, regular words such as *boy*, *help*, and *sad*. Keeping the base words simple helps children focus on learning the inflections as opposed to becoming distracted by unfamiliar words.

For students who have mastered the basic inflectional morphemes, teachers can select beginning-level derivational morphemes (*pre*, *non*). In general, suffixes are more easily grasped than prefixes and roots. Students already have a schema for dealing with suffixes because they attach to even the most basic words in the English language. Students who speak other Latinate languages such as French or Spanish will also understand the importance of suffixes because in these languages, the suffix often determines the masculine or feminine form of a word.

After introducing new morphemes, students should have opportunities to work with manipulatives to combine morphemes, thus creating new words. To do this, the morphemes you teach should build on each other. In a middle school sixth-grade class, for example, the first group of morphemes presented in the fall might include the roots *port* and *trans*. Children already know some basic affixes, like *de*, *re*, *ing*, and *ed*. You might at this time introduce—or allow students to add—*fer* and *ient*. In this case, manipulatives might look like this:

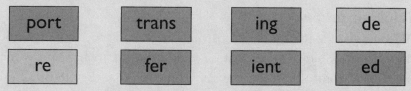

Children can move these around to make numerous words: *transport, deport, report, transfer, transient, transporting, reported,* and so on. In doing so, they should jot down their words on a piece of paper. Making lists of words helps students to begin to see relationships among the words they've created. The color-coding helps children to visualize the word parts:

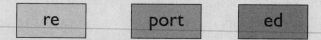

When the next set of morphemes is introduced (I recommend doing this biweekly), students should be able to recycle some of the morphemes they have already learned. In this example, the teacher might add *scrib/scribe/script, circum, pre,* and *sub*. Now the following manipulatives will be added:

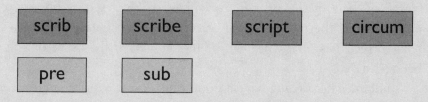

Students may now use these morphemes, as appropriate, with previously learned morphemes. Even though using the new morphemes alone can help children make *circumscribe, prescribe, subscribe, prescript,* and so on, students might also make *subscribed* or *prescribed*.

(Continued)

In the course of this process, teachers can encourage students to add morphemes that they already know to make words. In this case, students might already know *ion* and be able to make *subscription*, for example. Encouraging students to access prior knowledge in the new context of morpheme manipulatives affords them the opportunity to look at familiar words in a new way.

Differentiation

Although you may plan direct instruction around specific morphemes, this does not necessarily mean that all children need to have the same morphemes in front of them at the same time, or that they must all use their morpheme manipulatives to the same end. For learners who still struggle with inflection, it is important to keep the inflectional morphemes in play so that they continue to practice, even though you may be introducing derivations to the class. The morpheme manipulatives example includes inflections (*ed*, *ing*) in addition to derivations (*re*, *de*).

Students who are learning English as a new language—or any students who need additional support with transferring vocabulary knowledge into their reading and writing—will benefit from having access to morpheme or word lists when they are reading and writing. This can be accomplished easily if students have a writing journal—the lists may simply be taped into the front and back covers. Students will have ready access to them when they are writing, and they will be able to see their word lists grow over the course of the semester or year. You might consider setting up a system to tally the times they use the word correctly in their writing. After ten or fifteen correct uses, that word can be highlighted in the list as one that has been mastered.

Students who already have a good grasp on the morphemic structure of language still need opportunities to play with language structure and to learn new morphemes. However, if you find that some kids are quickly exhausting the possible word combinations with the morphemes you've taught, you can up the ante a bit. Not only will these students benefit from access to additional morphemes that you provide but you can also challenge them to use words they know to add morphemes on their own.

In her ninth-grade classroom in Virginia, Mrs. Brewick is talking to her students about the words they have made using their morpheme manipulatives. Sara, a shy blonde girl who likes to read, has just offered up a word for discussion:

"So, you gave me the word *subscription*," says Mrs. Brewick, "which uses the root *script*, or *scribe*. Let's walk through the morphological definition together." She writes the word on the chalkboard.

"Well, *sub* sounds like the first part of submarine. And I think it means below or under," Sara suggests. Mrs. Brewick circles *sub* and draws a line out from the circled portion of the word. On it she writes *under*.

"Any thoughts on the other parts of the word?"

Juan, an astute student, adds, "We just learned that *script* means to write, so maybe it has something to do with writing under something." Mrs. Brewick circles *script* and again notes the meaning.

"Like on the computer. You can check the subscript box, and the text is a little lower than the line," Casey, a self-proclaimed computer programmer, suggests.

"That's a good connection. OK, so we think that *subscript* means to write below or under. Let's put these definitions in the same order as the morphemes in the word. *Subscript* would then mean to underwrite. Has anyone heard another meaning for the term *underwrite*?"

"When my parents bought our house, they had to go through an underwriting process to get the loan." Michael says a little uncertain that he is on the right path.

"So that process had something to do with money, right?"

"Yes, I guess so," Michael continues.

"Great. So we have another possible meaning on the table—it could mean to provide money for something. How would that fit with the idea that you subscribe to a magazine or a newspaper?"

"Well, for my *Sports Illustrated* I pay the money for the subscription in advance. So in a way, I am giving them the money they need to make the magazine before they actually make it." Matt chimes in.

"Yes. That's true. So we might say that a subscription is supporting something with a guarantee of money. As a point of clarification, does anyone remember what *ion* marks?"

"It marks a noun with a condition or action," Sara says. "We learned that last year."

"Excellent."

Through this conversation with kids, Mrs. Brewick has helped them to unpack the word meaning through morphology. Because students were able not only to give the "definitions" for various morphemes but also make connections to other areas of life—technology, magazines—Mrs. Brewick gauges that their understanding of this particular word is solid.

Effective use of morpheme manipulatives relies on both the opportunity to physically manipulate word parts in an effort to make connections among words, and the following conversation that walks students through the morphological thinking behind each word, allowing them to approximate a definition.

Morpheme Squares

Morpheme Squares, another activity that allows students to physically manipulate morphemes, encourages them to play with words while attempting to solve a puzzle with a concrete solution. Morpheme Squares are similar to the puzzles you might find in toy stores that work to build a square puzzle by connecting pictures. These puzzles might show half of a frog, for example, on each side of a square puzzle piece (either the top half or the bottom half). The object is to combine all of the squares in the puzzle into a larger square so that when complete, each frog will have a head and a body. Morpheme Squares carry the same objective. Each side of a square puzzle piece is labeled with a morpheme that children work to match up with another morpheme on another square. In the end, the student has created one large square puzzle, with each of the morphemes matched up with another to create a real word (see Figure 2.1).

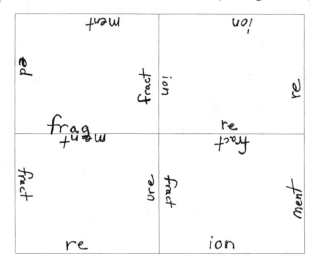

Figure 2.1   *4-Square Morpheme Square*

Setup

Just as with Morpheme Manipulatives, students can make their own Morpheme Squares or teachers can create stock sets. Either way, the setup is the same. First, determine how complicated you want the puzzles to be. The most basic structure includes four squares.

Each added set of squares makes the puzzle significantly more complex. For this reason, I often use rectangular puzzles as well, allowing me to add only two additional squares at a time instead of enforcing a square shape that will require the addition of five or more additional pieces. Here is a sample I created using six boxes:

aqua	tic	duce
duce	re	duce
aque	duct	re
duce	duct	aqu
de	con	atic
re	duct	naut
pro	aqua	atic
pro	arium	duce

Next, make a template. (Templates for four- and six-square puzzles are in Appendix A.) I simply insert a blank table into a Word document. Before I had computer access, I used a ruler and marker to do this by hand. If students are creating their own puzzles, simply provide them with a blank template and ask them to write in morphemes by hand. If you are creating the puzzle, you can either use text boxes to add the morphemes to the template in a Word document, or you can write the morphemes into the boxes by hand.

To solve the puzzle, students cut apart the template and try to reconstruct the puzzle. Be forewarned (and forewarn your students!) that this is not as easy as it may seem. Before you give a new puzzle to your students, try it yourself to ensure that it is within their range.

STEP INTO A CLASSROOM

Tracy has five minutes before the bell rings to dismiss her fourth-block class on a Monday afternoon. Earlier in the block, she introduced two new roots (*graph/gram*, *photo*) and two new affixes (*ic*, *able*) to her seventh-grade students. She has the following list of morphemes, which students have copied into their agendas, on her chalkboard: *graph/gram*, *photo*, *tele*, *bio*, *auto*, *ing*, *y*, *ic*, *able*, and *er*. She distributes a Morpheme Square template with nine boxes and tells her students to make a puzzle for homework. She reminds them that if they wish to combine morphemes, they must indicate the morphemes separately and use a plus sign (*graph + y*, *graph + ing*). They are to cut their puzzles into pieces and bring the pieces in a sandwich bag to the next class. Kevin makes the puzzle shown in Figure 2.2.

On Wednesday when students arrive in Tracy's class, they trade their puzzles and spend their "Do Now" time (the first few minutes of class) attempting to put together a classmate's puzzle. Today Tracy asks them to rotate puzzles by handing them to the person on their left. At other points in the year, Tracy has asked students to put all of their puzzles in a basket, and she has randomly distributed them. Often Tracy pairs students at roughly the same level for a six-week grading term and has them swap puzzles only with each other, allowing her to differentiate as needed.

Although this may look like a simple game to a passerby, because the outside perimeter of the puzzle also includes morphemes, students will initially find many morpheme combinations that make viable words but that won't actually solve the larger puzzle. She has challenged her students to combine and recombine morphemes to solve the puzzle. Tracy knows that most of the students

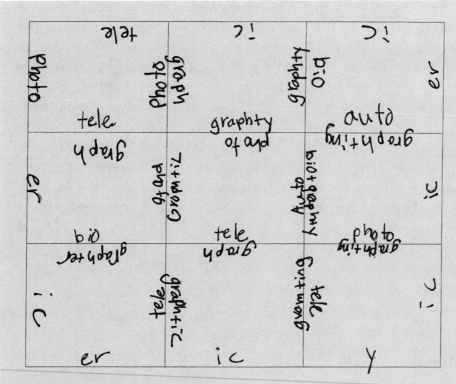

Figure 2.2 *Morpheme Square 9-Square*

won't solve the puzzle today, but she understands that this practice time spent manipulating taught morphemes will help her students to better understand their meaning and their possible combinations.

As a portion of tonight's homework, Tracy will challenge students to solve their own puzzles and to make a list of words using the morphemes. This will provide additional practice time and will also elicit a student-generated list of known words that use the morphemes she's taught.

Differentiation

Aside from creating leveled groups of students and asking them to use morphemes that fit with their understanding, teachers can also differentiate this game by simply changing the number of boxes in the puzzle. This way, all students practice with the same morphemes, but the output quantity has changed.

Teachers may also elect to brainstorm a list of words as a class and allow some students to use that list when creating their Morpheme Squares. When using this option, the list may be written with or without morpheme separation (*photo-graph* vs. *photograph*). Each of these options provides a different level of scaffolding. Is this fair, you wonder? Well, wasn't part of the objective the production of words? Absolutely. Remember that these puzzles will be cut into parts, and students will need to construct the words again. When they are reconstructing the words, you can choose whether they will use the word list to help, depending on what you know of your students' needs. Providing a word list initially will help students to recall possible combinations, which is particularly helpful for English Language Learners and students with learning disabilities.

Morpheme Walls

Word walls reinforce word study and make available a bank of words that students have already worked with and now own. Many word walls contain random lists of words that are related only because they were found in the same text. Morpheme Walls, however, are created around word parts. This method encourages students to continually build words using the morphemes they have studied, and to deconstruct unknown words when they encounter them in text and in conversation.

Setup

Like morpheme manipulatives, effective Morpheme Walls are color-coded (and even cooler, color-coded to match your class' morpheme manipulatives). When choosing a spot for your Morpheme Wall, make sure that you've selected a wall—or a portion of a wall—that is easily accessible and visible to all students.

Make signs to designate spaces for prefixes, roots, and suffixes. Again, the color coding should be consistent. You may also want to include a section of "Words We Know." As you introduce new morphemes, use appropriately color-coded index cards on which to write the morphemes as you add them to the wall. Alternatively, you can ask your students to write the

STEP INTO A CLASSROOM

On this hot August day, the sun shines through the windows of Ms. Kelly's room. Her seventh-grade students are still abuzz with summer stories even though it is already the second full week of the school year. Last week, Ms. Kelly introduced morpheme study to her students, explaining that this would be a portion of their vocabulary work.

In this school system, students in seventh grade work a great deal with the concept of change and continuity, exploring across the curriculum the ways things change over time and how things can remain the same. So Ms. Kelly started their morpheme study with the root *migr* (to move). As a class, they generated a list of words that contain the featured root. Then using morpheme manipulatives, students began to deconstruct and reconstruct the words on their list. In Ms. Kelly's class, students use cut strips of paper for their manipulatives, and Ms. Kelly uses the same colors of paper (which she feeds through her computer printer) to create the Morpheme Wall. In this case, prefixes are on yellow paper, roots are on red paper, and suffixes are on blue paper.

At the beginning of the week, Ms. Kelly had put a sheet of red paper with the root *migr* and several words using that root on the class Morpheme Wall. As the week progressed and students worked with their manipulatives, Ms. Kelly began to encourage students to add words to their wall.

This week Ms. Kelly has introduced *corp* (body). This root takes several different spellings, so she has scaffolded students by including all of the spellings on the header for this section of the Morpheme Wall. Students have begun adding their words, just as they had in the previous week. Figure 2.3 shows what the Morpheme Wall looks like at this point in the year.

Notice that the Morpheme Wall is still quite small. As students become more confident with word structures, the number of words for each root will likely grow. Additionally, as students find words using previously studied roots in their reading, they will be able to add them.

In the close-up photo (Figure 2.4), notice, too, that Ms. Kelly has scaffolded students by providing sample words on each of the section headers. These will be removed quickly, forcing students to generate word lists on their own. *(Continued)*

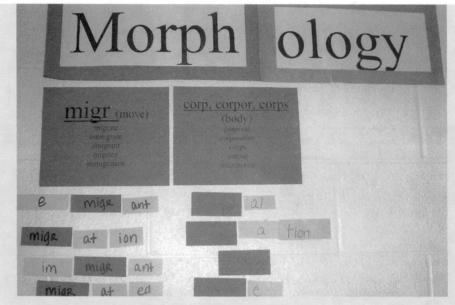

Figure 2.3   *Morpheme Wall—Week Two*

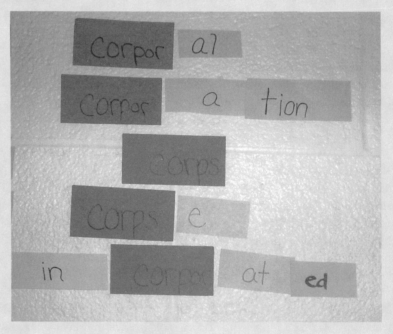

Figure 2.4   *Morpheme Wall—Week Two (close-up)*

A few weeks later, I visit Ms. Kelly's class again. It is now the fifth week of school, and the Morpheme Wall in her room continues to expand (see Figure 2.5). In the last few weeks Ms. Kelly has introduced *phob* (fear), *fract/frag* (to break or bend), and *graph* (to write).

Here you can see that the Morpheme Wall is expanding. Due to limited space, Ms. Kelly will rotate morphemes off the wall at the end of each quarter. Because of this, students also keep lists in their writing journals, using one page for each root. This gives them access to the words throughout the year.

In this closer photo (Figure 2.6), it's easy to see that Ms. Kelly has already removed the scaffolding of providing words on the root sheets she uses as section headers. Although students still generate a list together as a class, that list must come entirely from their own lexicons. Just like the early weeks of school, the students use morpheme manipulatives before putting words on the Morpheme Wall. This helps them to continue to play with the structure of language.

Figure 2.5 *Morpheme Wall—Week Five* (*Continued*)

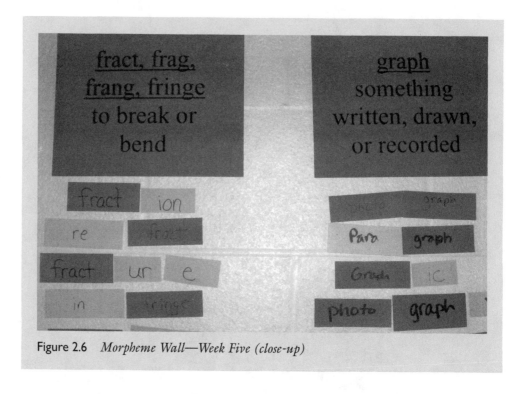

Figure 2.6 *Morpheme Wall—Week Five (close-up)*

morphemes on index cards and attach them to the wall as they are learned. It is helpful if you can make all (or even most) of your morpheme cards at one time and have them laminated so you can use them repeatedly.

Morpheme Walls should be fluid spaces that change and grow as students learn additional morphemes. If you are including a "Words We Know" section, it should also be fluid and, most important, student generated. Encourage kids to add words they generate through other morpheme strategies, such as morpheme manipulatives. As students incorporate words from the "Words We Know" section into their speech and writing, move them into a file box, allowing space for new words but still allowing easy access to the known words.

Differentiation

Over time, word walls can become overwhelming with morphemes and words beginning to overlap each other and begin to appear cluttered. This can be distressing for some students, particularly for those with learning disabilities. For this reason, you may wish to remove morphemes at specified intervals throughout the year (each marking period, as students master them, or even monthly), thus making the wall less cluttered. If you use this approach, ensure that students know which morphemes will be coming down and when. Give students a chance to write these morphemes in a journal so they have continued access to them.

Another way to differentiate instruction around the Morpheme Wall is to include the meaning with the morpheme as you add it to your wall (*pre/before*). This will provide scaffolding for students who need additional time to master new morphemes. Eventually, these cards can be swapped out for cards without the meaning included as all students master them and as you see transfer of their understanding into their writing. You can keep the scaffolded cards sorted alphabetically in index card boxes.

To challenge more advanced students, combine your word wall with a "graffiti" component (see Figure 2.7). Put butcher paper up before you add

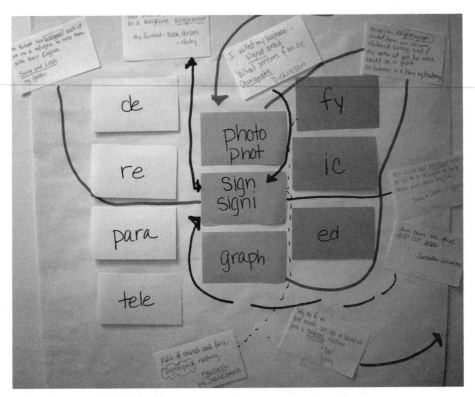

Figure 2.7 *Graffiti Wall*

morphemes to the wall. Instead of a teacher-created "Words We Know" section, allow students to write words that include the displayed morphemes on the butcher paper. When using this adaptation, encourage your students to include excerpts from their own or others' writing, highlighting the words that use the displayed morphemes. You can also have them connect their words back to the morphemes used.

In Figure 2.7 you can see that students have just begun their Graffiti Wall for the year, but the morpheme component encourages them to think about word parts as they encounter words in their reading.

Another strategy to encourage students to think about and manipulate word parts is sorting and re-sorting.

Sort and Re-sort

Typical word sorts require students to sort words according to word features (typically spelling patterns), physically placing all of the words containing *ee*, for example, in one place. As students move beyond the initial stages of word study (phonemic awareness and letter naming) and begin working with word patterns, inflections, and derivations (morphemes that alter a word's meaning), it is important that we also ask students to re-sort words for a variety of purposes.

For example, a typical word sort might look like this:

ee	ea	ĕ
beet	beat	bet
see	seat	set
meet	meat	met

In this example, words are sorted according to the spelling patterns *ee*, *ea*, and *ĕ*. Students completing this sort are working with word patterns, not word meanings.

Once students reach derivational constancy (the final stage of word study in which words are analyzed for their morphemic structure), though, teachers have more options. For example, an initial sort might look like this:

port	tract	voke
report	detract	revoke
purport	subtract	provoke
deport	protract	invoke
support	retract	
import		

Using this kind of sort, students categorize words according to their roots—that is, all of the *port* words are together. But students could also be asked to sort these words according to prefix—such a re-sort will help them to understand that each of these words is made by combining two morphemes. In addition, because some of the prefixes have multiple spellings, a re-sort will help students to relate those multiple spellings. Such a re-sort might look like this:

re	pro/pur	de	sub/sup	im/in
report	purport	deport	support	import
retract	protract	detract	subtract	
revoke	provoke			invoke

Setup

Although there are books available that include premade word sorts, if you want them to match the morphemes you are teaching, you will need to either adapt the premade sorts or create your own. Creating sorts does take time, but you will marvel at the positive effect they have on your students' understanding.

The easiest way to make sorts is to create them as a table in a word-processing document. Once printed, you can make copies to distribute to students, and they can cut apart the columns and rows before sorting.

Another alternative is to have students keep their own collection of note cards including all of the words you've studied together in an alphabetized index card box, and for you to tell them which words to pull for a sort with a particular objective. This task will require students to make note cards as new words are formed with the morphemes they are studying. For those teachable moments that arise during discussion, having a stash of little sticky notes will allow you to quickly accomplish a sort. (Larger sticky notes can be cut into strips, thus maximizing their space and use.) Distribute a stack of sticky notes to each child and have students write one word per sticky note. Then kids can quickly sort the words by manipulating the notes into rows and columns on their desks.

Differentiation

Obviously, the fewer the words and morphemes, the easier the sorting process becomes. To make the sort more difficult, ask more advanced students to add words they know that use the same roots as the words you've included. More advanced students will be able to create categories for any additional morphemes used as well. In the sample sort, students might add suffixes as a sorting category, for example.

You will also need to decide whether you will provide students with the category headings (in the table on page 39, these are the bolded morphemes). Giving students the category headings makes the sort easier than if they must determine the categories on their own.

Start the sort process by reading the words to be sorted to your students. This will ensure that everyone has heard the correct pronunciation for each word. Then, ask your students to sort the words according to root (review the roots and their meanings first, if necessary). After students have completed this initial sort, ask them to share with a partner or small group their word groupings and their thinking behind the grouping.

As a class, review the correct word groupings and discuss the thinking behind the categories created, if necessary. After this review, students should write a sentence capturing their thought process, which will help to solidify their understanding of the roots used. Then ask students to re-sort the words according to another morpheme—prefix, suffix, or combining form. Again, have students share their groupings and the thinking behind them, review as a class, and ask students to write.

Finally, ask students if they can come up with another way to sort the words. If they can, continue with the same process until the various possibilities for sorting words are exhausted. The more complex the words, the more ways there are to sort them.

Students who need additional scaffolding will benefit from using a matrix to record their sorted words. For example:

	port	**tract**	**voke**
re	report	retract	revoke
pro/pur	purport	protract	provoke
de	deport	detract	
sub/sup	support	subtract	
im/in	import		invoke

Although this strategy takes time to front-load (or preteach), sorting and re-sorting yields significant gains for student learning as kids begin to internalize word patterns and word relationships. The ability to identify and classify multiple morphemes in a word demonstrates deeper understanding than simply sorting words based on one morpheme alone.

Twist and Flip—Word Manipulations

Remember when the newspaper had anagrams in the puzzle section? An anagram, you'll remember, is a word game that involves taking a discrete word or phrase and rearranging its letters to form a new word or phrase. After reading the comics each Sunday afternoon, I would attempt the word puzzles, often having to look at the answers but always enjoying the challenge. Using several variations of the anagram game in the classroom provides students the opportunity to manipulate portions of a word to create something new. The simplest version requires students to manipulate a single letter, following a distinct spelling pattern—for example, *cat* becomes *hat* becomes *mat* becomes *sat*. Taking that one step further, students might replace a single letter to form a new pattern—for example, *cat* becomes *cap* becomes *sap* becomes *sam* becomes *ham* becomes *hat*.

More advanced word manipulations require students to replace one or more letters with multiple letters—for example, *cat* becomes *catch* becomes *match* becomes *watch* becomes *wash* becomes *smash*. In another version of the game, students scramble the letters in a word or phrase to create different words—for example, *slip* becomes *lips*, or *spot* becomes *stop*.

Another activity that challenges students to play with words and word formations is working with nonsense words. Lewis Carroll's "The Jabberwocky" provides a context and an example for students to begin nonsense word play.

STEP INTO A CLASSROOM

Students arrive in Bob's eighth-grade English class to find the following written on the board:

"Create an anagram sequence starting with the word *song* and ending with *spoke*. Share your anagram sequence with a partner."

Before the tardy bell begins to ring, students are hard at work, trying to solve the word puzzle before Bob can finish taking the roll. Because Bob uses these puzzles on a regular basis, students know that they can change the order of letters or substitute letters one "move" at a time. (Earlier in the year, Bob put the rules on the board above the word puzzle.) After a few minutes, Paul and Danny each have a sequence, and they begin to share.

Paul	Danny
song	song
strong	sock
string	stock
strike	stoke
stroke	spoke
spoke	

Bob moves around the room, looking at the students' work. He notices that Paul's and Danny's lists are quite different and asks them about their thought processes. Paul says, "I worked on the beginning of the word first, trying to get from s to sp before taking on the end of the word. But it didn't work. Halfway through, I saw that I could change the ending from ng to ke and be almost there."

Danny responds saying, "I tried to use as few steps as possible. It got hard when I got to *stock*, though. I had to get a dictionary to see if *stoke* really is a word, which it is."

Bob says, "I can tell you were really thinking about how words work and which letter combinations might help to solve this puzzle. Good job using the dictionary to check *stoke*, too." Pleased with the boys' excellent thinking, Bob moves to another pair of students. It doesn't matter that Danny's and Paul's word sequences are different or that they used a different number of steps to complete the challenge. What matters is that both boys are able to distinguish between the word parts that they altered to reach their conclusions.

The Jabberwocky

This activity earned me the nickname "Psycho" for a while among the freshmen of Fayette High School. Our school had just opened four new computer labs—gleaming with state-of-the-art Macintosh 2es—remember those blocky, beige monitors? When I think of the relative limitations of these clunky machines as compared to the many tricks and vast memory of today's tiny iPod, I laugh. Still, at the time, we were thrilled. The labs came to us as part of a grant that required English teachers to spend one-quarter of class time in the labs, with students working on computers. Part of what we hoped to achieve in the labs was for students to develop some basic computer skills while practicing components of the language arts curriculum.

In an effort to make the language arts portion of the work meaningful and not to simply spend our time in the lab puttering with the computers, I had the notion to upload "The Jabberwocky" and have students highlight, boldface, underline, and italicize the various parts of speech. Of course they would be learning how to use these features in Microsoft Word as well— two birds with one stone, I thought. Yes, we could have accomplished this task much more easily with a bunch of highlighters and paper, but that wouldn't have met the grant criteria. So, off to the computer lab we went.

At first the kids thought the exercise would be a breeze. How hard is it, really, to italicize something? But it only took moments for Jerry to ask, "What does *brillig* mean?" No one knew. Bailey grabbed a dictionary. No luck. Then Pam added, "Hey, what's *mome*?" Again, Bailey flipped through that trusty dictionary. Again, no luck. "That psycho has us working with fake words!" Clay jumped in.

But there was a method to my madness. When students work with nonsense words, they have to examine carefully both the words' parts and how the words are functioning in the sentence to determine the part of speech. These high school freshmen hadn't learned that the final morpheme of a word determines its part of speech. In fact, they had almost no knowledge of word structures. While they could have identified all of the prepositions in a paragraph, it was only because they had been forced to memorize the list in eighth grade, not because they deeply understood structures of English.

While my original Jabberwocky activity could not have been called a great success, it did provide me with food for thought. Lewis Carroll's complex poem used morphemes the students had never been exposed to before. What would happen, I wondered, if I asked the students to write their *own* nonsense poems? Then, they could trade with a partner and decode each other's work! Students naturally used morphemes that they knew well to write their nonsense poems, so the process of decoding them not only was easier but also reinforced work we'd done with those morphemes as a class.

Setup

Before you start this activity, it is helpful to review inflections and parts of speech you've studied with your students. Remind them that morphemes can be simple but still pack a meaningful punch—for example, when my daughter sees a pile of dolls, she would like for them to be the *girl's* dolls and not the *girls'* dolls!

Next, ask your students to generate a list of nonsense words and to then classify them by part of speech. How do they know they are correct? Can they approximate the word meanings?

STEP INTO A CLASSROOM

Joy is preparing her students to write nonsense poems. After using the class Morpheme Wall to review morphemes students have studied, Joy asked the kids to make lists of nonsense words for homework. As class began on this snowy March day, Joy asked students to write their lists on one of the four chalkboards around her classroom.

Lucy's list includes *frolickig*. As Joy circulates around the room, she noticed the word and asks Lucy about it. "What part of speech do you think that word is?"

"It's a noun."

"How do you know?"

"I think the *ig* is a noun ending, right? And it sounds a little like *frolic*, meaning merry or glad. So it might mean that it's the time of frolicking—or a time for being glad."

"That's a pretty awesome word," Joy compliments. "It uses a really descriptive and strong word as a base."

After circulating and asking students about their word lists, Joy facilitates a brief class discussion and then says, "We are going to use your nonsense words to write nonsense poems similar to a poem by Lewis Carroll called 'The Jabberwocky.' Listen as I read this poem aloud." As Joy reads, the kids giggle at the ridiculous poem. When she finishes reading, she says, "So, using the words on the chalkboards, work with a partner to write a poem that combines nonsense words and 'real' words. You will also need to include the poem's 'translation.'"

A Student Sample

Megan is a sixth-grade student who struggles with reading. Although she can decode common monosyllabic words, she often fails when she attempts to decode multisyllabic words. Mr. Brown, her teacher, has been working with Megan to understand that words are constructed of parts that form patterns. He challenges Megan to make up words using parts of words she already knows. After doing this, she creates the poem shown in Figure 2.8.

To create new words, Megan began with words she already knows—*fur, jump, eat, sit, toy*—and added new endings. Interestingly, some of the added endings would be more typical of Spanish (*aro*) than English (*ful*), and her use of suffixes (in English the final suffix determines the part of speech) doesn't always align with the part of speech for the translation (*happiful* would be an adjective, but Megan uses it as a verb). Still, Megan

Figure 2.8 *Nonsense Poem—Dogie*

demonstrates an understanding of the morphemic structure of language in the way she breaks apart and reconstructs words.

Daisy takes a more sophisticated approach with her poem (see Figure 2.9).

Nonsense Words

snootelfluff—fuzzy flower petals used to tickle dragons
zafuzzle—a big question
myneley—an exclamation meaning "Oh! Dear!"
rindel—enormous hope
heluzip—big trouble
uzzy—foggy and misty
snoap—slippery slope
thirpda—chirping sound
roddel—bumpy old road
smale—shelled bug
Trisai—a dragon's name
expudle—mist rising off puddles
Zantia—a mystical island
Zoonies—Zantian woodland creatures
flutle—curvy fluted loops

"Zafuzzle"

Thirpda noises ring—
Could they be Zoonies?
Or Trisai?

Meandering down the uzzy roddel
Expudle rising
Making Zantia magical.
Will Trisai appear?

Rindel

Zafuzzle

Flower flutles mingle in the air
Snootelfluff flies
Up! Up!

Ah-choo!
Trisai!

Is he near?

Figure 2.9 *Student Nonsense Poem*

Here we see a better command of the morphemic structure, with parts of speech for created words aligning to parts of speech of the "real" English words in the translation. In addition, Daisy constructs complex words (*expudle*) by combining Latin roots and affixes rather than relying on adding inflections to Anglo-Saxon words, as seen in the previous example.

In Summary

Each of these strategies helps students to manipulate and play with various morphemes. The goal isn't for your students to achieve a perfect understanding of morphemic structure, but rather for them to begin to develop an understanding of and a genuine curiosity about word structures and word parts. When this goal is accomplished through play, students are more likely to employ morphemic strategies when they encounter unknown words because they know that words are related to other words and that all words are formed around patterns.

Etymological Clues  *3*

Language is dynamic, reflecting cultural and individual change. When we help students to understand how etymology plays into morphemic structure and to our use of words, their understanding is enhanced and their curiosity is stimulated. Because language is evolving all of the time, new words are constantly entering into the lexicon. When I was a child, technology consisted of televisions, phones, SLR (single-lens reflex) cameras, and so on. I remember our first gigantic VCR, getting cable television for the first time, early desktop computers, and cell phones that were the size of shoes. With each of these inventions came new terminology. Some of the words already existed in our world—*mouse*, for example—but they took on new meanings. Other brand-new words, like *Internet*, quickly became infused into everyday language.

New words enter the language for several reasons. Some, like *lasagna*, enter via immigration and an influx of other languages. Technological advances create the need for new words, like *laser*. Some new words come into popular use because someone simply made them up and they stuck, like *bling*. At the same time, the meanings of existing words may change or evolve, and other words may become obsolete (*betwixt*).

So what is etymology exactly? At its root, *etymology* breaks down like this: *etymos* meaning *true* and *logos* meaning *word*. So through etymological study, we are attempting to uncover the true sense of words. When we know a bit about the origin of words or parts of words, we develop a deeper understanding of language—the words we learn are more meaningful and resonant.

Students will be fascinated by how their own understanding of even the most common words can change as they learn more about etymology. Dr. Rollin David Larrick (teacher, linguist, and founder of the innovative vocabulary program Dynamic Literacy) provides a wonderful example of how deconstructing words and looking into the origins of morphemes add depth to our understanding.

"The morphological definition is usually understandable," states Dr. Larrick, "but it will differ from actual current usage because words change over time. Think about the word *obvious*. If you ask students what this word means, they will say, 'Well, it's right there,' or something to that effect. But the morphological definition is different. *Ob* means *in the way*, *vi* means *road*, and *ous* means *full of*. So morphologically, *obvious* means *full of in the way of the road*. So it is something that is right there—in the way. This discussion with kids will take nonsensical morphological meaning and make sense of it."

Dr. Larrick continues, "Some words are more metaphorical—although all words are metaphorical in a way. Think about the word *companion*. If you break that word down, you get *com* meaning *with* or *together* and *pan* meaning *bread*. So a companion is someone with whom you break bread. If you take the time to explain this, kids will get the metaphorical piece of the word and leap to, 'If you break bread with them, you probably would do just about everything with them.' When we use both the morphological definition and the dictionary definition, kids can watch meanings change. They really get a sense of language that way. We need to do both because they reinforce each other."

The best part about teaching etymology is that kids already have a conceptual understanding of it, even if they don't know what it is. Think about the newly invented language of text messaging. Teens helped to create and certainly to perpetuate its use, understanding that they are "speaking" a language most adults don't understand. Because of this, kids already know that language changes. In this case, typing every letter of a word impeded the speed necessary to keep up in chat rooms and that evolved into the "texting" that kids do today on their cell phones (LOL/laugh out loud).

Kids also know that language can be invented, or that meanings of familiar words can be changed. When I was in high school, one of the games various groups of students played was making up a word or phrase—or a new meaning for a word or phrase—and using it just to see how long it took before someone outside the group used it. I'm quite certain this is actually a rite of passage among high school students because years later when I became a teacher, my own students engaged in the same game. In my generation's case, words like *cool,* meaning interesting and great (not chilly) and phrases like *What's the diff?* became commonplace. Today students use words like *bling, texting,* and *pac-manning* (driving on the dotted lane divider) as well as phrases like, *Peace out* and *Check your vitals* (meaning to check email, websites, etc.).

Many kids also know that slang may (or may not) evolve into full-fledged words that earn inclusion in *Webster's.* I think every kid in the English-speaking world gave some adult an I-told-you-so glare when *ain't* finally made the list—even if the definition acknowledges that the term is slang. The word *slang* itself bids intrigue. Over time this word has been associated with thieves or ne'er-do-wells, claiming that they had their own special language (mid-1700s) and jargon related to a trade (early 1800s). The exact origin is unknown. Some sources relate it to words meaning *nickname* and others to roots meaning *abuse*—in this case, abuse of language. Still others believe it's related to *sling* (as in to *sling* something across a room), so in a sense, slinging language. Each of these associations provides clues to the word's connotations through time. Let's face it, a nickname is much nicer than abuse, but both elements are part of the word's meaning.

While most students understand the concept that language changes through the development of new meanings and additional words, they often don't know that words—and entire languages—can also become obsolete. This concept is hard to grasp. We are accustomed to new "stuff" being created all of the time—buildings, cars, and even words—but once the new building is in place, we quickly forget the one that was demolished. The same is true of words. *Betwixt* evolved into *between,* and now aside from the occasional glance at an older text, no one even remembers *betwixt.* Once a word falls out of common use, it is easy to forget it ever existed. If we needed a word for something at some point, how could we ever *not* need that word?

An even more perplexing thought to most English speakers is the notion that entire languages can die. We say that Latin is a "dead" language, and yet it is the foundation of so much of English. Truly, while not spoken anymore, Latin does still exist on paper, so we have a record of its history. But some dialects of languages and even entire languages truly die, leaving no record whatsoever. In 2004, the last speaker of Nushu (a Chinese female-specific language) died and took the language with her (*China Daily* 2004). In this particular tribe, ancient women developed a language that they passed on only orally to their daughters. The women never spoke the language in the company of men, and they never wrote it down. Thus, when the last speaker, who had no female descendents, died, so did the language.

Today, Native American tribes actively work to prevent the same fate for their many languages. The Native Languages of the Americas website (www.native-languages.org) is devoted to keeping more than 800 indigenous languages alive. Why? Because largely, English is spoken in lieu of these languages. Today's youth have no need for Arawak, Macushi, or Karuk: Their peers speak English.

To help students understand this aspect of etymology, teachers can look to idioms for some assistance in illustrating how certain word usages change over time. For example, the idiom *he got his just deserts* provides an example of a word meaning that is obsolete except for use in this idiom. Here *desert* means something deserved, like a punishment or reward, and dates back to the thirteenth century. But this use of *desert* today is relatively limited to this phrase—we tend to use the word as a verb (*to desert one's troops*).

Idioms also help to engage students in the joy of etymology. Because they use idioms in their daily speech, students are often interested in learning more about their origins and are often shocked to learn how some phrases came about. In college, my drama professor explained the term *break a leg* comes from Elizabethan theater. The men wore tights, and when they bowed, they extended one leg in front and bent the back leg in an effort to reveal their toned leg muscles. Where the knee bent in the back leg was referred to as the "break" in the leg. So in theater, telling someone to *break a leg* is to wish them many bows. (In researching this term, I have found some mystery around its origin, and with kids, that leads to another discussion about word origins, nuances, and a world of possibility!)

Why Teach Etymology

Aside from being a great deal of fun, etymology provides clues to spelling and the original intent, or true sense, of words. While such study will certainly enhance understanding and even spelling (ask any of the spellers at the National Spelling Bee), it is particularly important when students are reading literature from other eras as meanings change. Learning to trace word meanings provides deeper insight to the authors' intentions.

Spelling

Because of my work on this text, watching this year's National Spelling Bee became an entirely different experience for me. My husband, who was trying hard to ignore the fact that I was *actually watching* such an event, started asking questions. "Why do they ask the language of origin anyway?" This was all I needed.

It was the ninth round, and the young lady at the microphone had asked the origin of *cyanophycean* (pronounced sigh-an-o-fish-an), to which the pronouncer responded "Greek and Greek" (meaning both the first part of the word—*cyan*—and the last part of the word—*phycean*—are from Greek).

"See, the word should start *cy*," I said, admitting that I had never heard this word before. "But without knowing that it is from Greek, it could start with *s*. And the last part won't start like *fish*," I added. "*Phy* is the Greek for the *f* sound—like in *physician*." All I got in response from my husband was an—admittedly well-deserved—eye roll. (I tried spelling the word and missed by two letters. There's always next year!)

In an earlier round, the word *abseil* was given. The pronouncer indicated that the word originally came from German but that we get it from French. This clue allowed the speller to eliminate options because as the word evolved, so did the spelling.

The following chart indicates *some* of the more common spelling rules for various origins of English words.

Language of Origin	English sound	Spelling	Example
Latin	/o͞o/	u	influence
	/k/	c	concur
	/gz/	x	exit
Greek	/k/	ch	character
	/f/	ph	physical
	/i/	y	synonym
French	/y/ + /ā/ —end of word	ier	dossier
	/ō/	eau	plateau
		eaux	Bordeaux
		au	chauffeur
	/et/	ette	banquette

Reading

Etymology also provides information about how words change in their meaning, often lending insight to a text. In Shakespeare's time, for example, paper was quite expensive, and many actors could not read. Unlike modern theatrical practice where every actor has a copy of an entire script, actors in the Lord Chamberlain's Men (the company with which Shakespeare performed) received only their part to study. This part was handed to them on a rolled-up piece of paper (much like a scroll); thus, actors received their "rolls/roles," or parts.

Word Origins

As seen in the previous examples, understanding word origins provides clues to spelling and original intent of words. Through studying word origins, students learn that not all words carry the same weight. For example, Anglo-Saxon words, once deemed filthy and used only by lower classes, still carry a sense of simplicity and lack of education. Without emphasizing it, our culture tends to view multisyllabic words and words from various languages as being more sophisticated. Which sounds most "cultured"— snacks, appetizers, antipasto, starters, hors-d'oeuvres? Can you guess which words come from the Anglo-Saxon?

As students work with translated text, particularly of ancient Greek origin, they must understand that the original intent of some words differs from contemporary definitions. For example, the word *form* today generally refers to something's outward shape. But in Greek, this word refers to both outward shape and inward essence. In ancient Greek, taking on the *form* of something meant to represent not only the outward but also the inward expression, the very core of something. Unlike the notion of spirits and ghosts, taking *form* was to possess all of the inward qualities and characteristics. The meaning in Greek goes deeper than it does in English.

Ideally, kids will study word origins as scholars do, through original text and with dictionaries from various time periods. With these materials, linguists study the words used in a text and compare those words and usages to dictionaries or other documents from the same time period. It helps if kids can open their minds and come to a text assuming they don't really know some of the words. This strategy mimics how linguists and anthropologists look at ancient writing (hieroglyphics) to determine patterns and, consequently, meanings.

In 2006, for example, archeologists discovered a tablet that is believed to be the oldest writing in the New World, in Mexico. The stone carries sixty-two symbols in rows, with some symbols being repeated. This mimics other writing systems. Today, scholars are actively working to solve the puzzle of the language.

When kids bring this attitude to a text from a different time period, they too can become experts in studying language and its changes.

Setup

If possible, obtain dictionaries from various time periods. Old dictionaries are often relatively cheap in used bookstores and, in actuality, are true treasures. Working with tangible materials will make the search for words more interesting than typing them into an online etymology database (although these exist and can be excellent tools). As kids scan pages seeking out the desired word, they come across other words used when the dictionary was published, helping them to better understand the constant flux in language rather than drastic overnight and holistic changes.

Books designed to trace etymology are also useful tools, as the same tactile search process occurs. And as another resource, students may wish to access online databases designed for this purpose. If online resources are the only tools available to you and your students, use those sites designed by scholars because they will provide more accurate information.

In Practice

Melissa's seventh-grade language arts class is studying change and continuity in language. Although they work daily with roots and affixes, Melissa wants them to understand also that language changes over time, not just because different affixes are attached to roots. Although this is not a new concept for her students, Melissa is aware that they have little understanding of how words are added to a language. To help them, she has cut out pictures of some modern inventions and collected some dictionaries from the 1950s and 1960s.

Working in small groups, the students have several pictures with which to work and two dictionaries from different decades (one from the 1950s and 1960s and one current volume). Keisha, Lindsay, Matt, and Manuel are going through their pictures. One is of a woman wearing a swimsuit, and Keisha says, "That's a tankini. I want one, but my mom won't let me have one until I'm in high school."

"What's a tankini?" Matt asks shrugging his shoulders and rolling his eyes.

"It's like a bikini, but the top is more like a tank top." Lindsay explains. "I'm pretty certain it's not going to be in any of those dictionaries, though. I remember seeing pictures of women who swam in the Olympics in the 1950s, and their swimsuits looked more like dresses."

Manuel looks in one dictionary and Keisha looks in the other. Neither dictionary includes the word. "So what should we write about *tankini*?" Manuel asks.

"I guess we just put that it isn't in either dictionary. So it must be newer than . . . what's the date on that dictionary, Manuel?" Matt asks.

"1998."

"So it's newer than 1998, and it is a *ladies'* swimsuit that has two pieces and the top is like a tank top."

"Yeah, but how did it get to be in our language? The origin must be English, but how was the word formed?" Keisha asks.

"Isn't it just a combination of *bikini* and *tank top*?" Lindsay questions.

"That would make sense," Manuel agrees. "So it's a combination of two existing words."

The students write their word-origin guesses on their papers and look at the next picture—of an iPhone.

Differentiation

If students struggle with the idea of word origins and language that seems foreign to them, you can expose students to similar tools and processes while working with contemporary terms (as with Melissa's students) and working as a class to walk through the investigation process. Mary's seventh-grade students, for example, are working with the newly coined term *voluntourism*, a term to describe travel opportunities that include a volunteer experience. As the world's often-overwhelming needs—medical care, safe drinking water, livable housing—have taken center stage in the media, concerts, benefits, and Hollywood, more and more people are using vacation time as an opportunity to volunteer in needy areas while still seeing another part of the world. Thus, this term was coined by combining *volunteer* and *tourism*.

Mary writes the term on the chalkboard and asks students to look up the definition in the dictionary. Surprise! It isn't there! Mary asks why. When Jerry, a fun-loving boy responds, "This dictionary isn't any good," Mary pulls out another, thicker dictionary and asks, "Do I have a volunteer to see if this dictionary has *voluntourism*?"

Kelsey, a good-natured redhead says, "I'll see, but I'm kind of guessing it isn't in that one either."

Mary uses this example to engage kids in an investigation of recently coined words and how those words came into existence.

Another strategy to help kids understand the evolution of language revolves around changes in word meanings rather than focusing entirely on word origins. Often kids will latch onto this activity because they can generate words within their context easily and extend that understanding to other words they encounter when reading.

National Treasure has become one of my favorite movies. Not only do I find the historical aspects of the story intriguing, I love the language usage and the main character's love of words—and history. The story revolves around the notion that the back of the Declaration of Independence contains an invisible treasure map, leading to artifacts of historical significance and material wealth. In the opening scene, Ben, the main character, discovers a poem, in this case also a riddle, on the stem of a pipe. In pondering the words, he encounters the word *iron*. The other characters take for granted the reference, but Ben begins to play with the word—iron gall ink, ironclad, cast in iron, and so on. Eventually, he concludes that it refers to something resolved, which leads to the Declaration of Independence. This play with multiple meanings, and connotation in particular, leads to an understanding of the text, and—movie spoiler coming up—ultimately to the treasure.

Connotation vs. Denotation

Etymology provides insight to the connotative (figurative) meanings of words over time, rather than relying solely on denotative (literal) definitions. Language would be much simpler without these nuances, but, alas, they are what distinguish the natives from the visitors. For example, when visiting France, one might be reluctant to refer to someone as a *paysan*, seeing as the word in English means *peasant*, which carries some negative connotations. What an insult! And yet, when the French refer to the region of their upbringing, they refer to themselves as *paysans*, saying *nous sommes des paysans*. In this connotation, the word carries much pride, indicating a sense of connection and heritage. And one might note the relationship of this word to the French word *pays*, meaning *country*.

In English, my favorite example is the word *spinster*. Asking students the meaning of the word generally results in some negative comment about an "old hag." How interesting that the word currently carries a relatively negative connotation. (Its denotation is "an unmarried woman past the common age for marrying.") The word originates from *spinnen* (Middle English) meaning to *spin*, plus the feminine suffix (*stere*). Initially, the word carried a positive connotation because a woman who could spin (and whose families could afford a spinning wheel) didn't need to marry. These women were able to support themselves, thus avoiding the servitude that marriage often brought about. Over time, however, as English-speaking cultures allowed women to work and to own land, a sense of partnership between the sexes emerged, thus changing the connotation of the word. If it was culturally acceptable to work and own land, why then wouldn't one marry? Could it be possible that all of those independent women of the Middle Ages actually wanted to marry but couldn't fathom obeying men? Or that in today's society, with all its show of equality, remaining unmarried now carries a negative stigma rather than a favorable one?

English is littered with connotative meanings that have changed over time. Teaching our students that they exist, first of all, and, second, how to think through the ways that various connotations play out in communication is a necessary step toward teaching students to be true owners of the words they see, hear, and use.

Idioms

Playing with idioms is a fun, engaging way to help students to better understand connotation. Unless one is describing a three-year-old child having a temper tantrum outside, for example, to *hit the road* means to *leave*! Students enjoy playing with such phrases, determining both their denotative and connotative meanings and comparing them.

Students also have a great time exploring idioms translated from other languages. I encountered this idea before I ever stepped into a classroom. During a college internship, I had a roommate from France. One day she asked me for directions to a nearby shopping center and expressed concern that she wouldn't be able to find where she needed to go. I replied that it would be a "piece of cake." Her confused expression indicated that, while she knew all of the words in the phrase, she didn't understand. After explaining what I meant, I asked her if the French have a phrase to indicate that something is really easy: *jeu pour un enfant*, she told me. A child's game. Of course, I could have suggested that she take "the scenic route"—or the French equivalent, *le chemin des écoliers*, the way of school children.

These plays on words and connotative meanings add an element of playfulness as students grapple with connotative meaning.

Setup

The most difficult part of teaching connotative meaning through etymology is identifying reliable and accurate sources of information. While there are several excellent books and websites (listed in the references), the best way to get students to truly understand is to invest in dictionaries published during various time periods. Unabridged dictionaries that include etymology also work, but I have found that this isn't as effective as asking students to look up the primary definition of a word in multiple dictionaries.

From a text to be studied (or just from words that you and your students find interesting) select four to six words for students to investigate. Break students into groups, and give each student in the group a different word (this can either be written on slips of paper or simply told to them). Ask students to write their initial understanding of the word, which will most likely be the contemporary connotation. Then ask students to use the available resources to research the various connotations their words have had over time.

In Practice

Like her classmates, Joann, a tenth-grade student, is looking at the word written on her paper—*raffle*. Earlier in the class, Ms. Baldwin, her teacher, distributed a sheet of paper to students. Each person in Joann's group of five students has a different word. The assigned task is to write the definition of the word from several of the dictionaries available in the classroom, noting the publication date of each dictionary as she works. First, she writes her own definition, or understanding, of the word's meaning.

Raffle: a game where players buy a ticket for a little bit of money in hopes of winning a big prize.

As she looks through dictionaries, she notes that all of the definitions say something about the sale of tickets for a chance to win something. Finding a dictionary that includes etymology, and relieved to have more information, she writes:

Raffle: from Middle English, a dice game, plundering

Raffle: from Middle French, also a dice game, literally meaning rake for a fire

Raffle: from Middle High German, rake for a fire, to snatch away

Joann thinks about this. When you rake a fire, it's like sweeping. Perhaps a raffle is really when one person sweeps up everything, or snatches the winnings.

After students share their words in small groups, Ms. Baldwin asks the students to open their books to a short story called "The Lottery."

"What do you think of when you think of a lottery?" Ms. Baldwin questions.

"Winning a lot of money!" Hector shouts. As the class laughs, Ms. Baldwin continues with, "So what do you think this story will be about?"

"Winning a lot of money!" Hector repeats.

As a class, they read and discuss Jackson's disturbing story in which the "winner" of the lottery is stoned to death, an old form of population control. The students are appalled.

"That's not cool," Mariah, ever concerned about human rights, complains. "That's so, so mean."

"Yes, I would agree. But the story's ending wouldn't be so shocking if Jackson had written and published it during the time period that such events actually took place. It's shocking because readers come to the text with a prediction based on the contemporary connotation of the title. But is a lottery really about winning?"

"No, it's a gamble, a chance," Melissa says.

"True. So did the author violate the definition of the word? Or did she rely on readers predicting based on contemporary connotations?" Ms. Baldwin questions.

"But it's still just wrong," Mariah complains.

"Yeah, but we *did* make a prediction. Man, was my prediction way off," Hector adds.

"And now that we have read the story, let's go back to some of the words you investigated earlier. How many of you thought that your words would have a positive connotation, something about winning or getting a good surprise?"

Joann studies the word on her paper. Yes, she had thought only about the winning side of a raffle. Although she had acknowledged the chance aspect of the word, her understanding was more around the winning. But in that one person sweeping away everything, everyone else lost. A little tentative and shy, Joann slowly raises her hand and shares her information with her classmates.

In Summary

Although etymology may seem daunting at first, once kids begin to play with word histories, it's hard to get them to stop. Words are, indeed, fascinating. And when we help kids to play with word histories, not only do they understand words in new ways, their interest in words increases.

Accessing Learned Vocabulary

4

Although students must gain knowledge of approximately 4,000 words per year *just to keep up* with what the next grade has to offer (Nagy and Anderson 1984), those new words mean little if students don't truly *own* them—meaning, they are able not only to understand words when heard or read but to use them correctly in their own speech and writing. Developing receptive vocabulary is helpful, but it is not enough to prepare students for the increasing demands of each grade level. We want our students to be able to produce rich vocabulary appropriate to the context and audience in which they are operating. For this to occur, students must have frequent opportunities to access rich vocabulary through word play activities. Word play activities challenge students to think beyond the language that they use every day, and encourage them to hone in on word structures and language patterns. This helps to cement students' understanding of new vocabulary.

Wordsters

Based on the Milton Bradley game of the same name, this adapted classroom activity can be used in several contexts: every day or sporadically; with the whole class, in groups, or in pairs. Not only is this game easy to set up, requiring minimal pre-teaching, it is just as easy to play. In the original game, players turn over a card to reveal a sequence of three letters. They then compete to see who, in a matter of only two minutes, can generate the most words that use the letters in sequence, but not necessarily grouped together.

Rules of Play

Write a set of three letters on the chalkboard or overhead projector. If you prefer, have your students each write the three letters on an index card. Next, students brainstorm as many words as they can, using those three letters in sequence—but not necessarily a *connected* sequence. For example, the letters *SPA* might lead to *space*, *spatial*, or *spatter*. But they could also lead to *special*, *superficial*, and *especially*. The letters appear in the same order in each word, but there may be other letters in between. Just like in the game Boggle, students earn one point for each word that is unique to their list—a word that no one else in the group has written. Depending on your class, allow between one and five minutes for "play" (generating a word list) with each letter combination.

Setup

The easiest way to incorporate Wordsters in the classroom is to make a set of index cards with combinations of three letters. Although you may choose to simply use the list in Appendix B, it's easier in practice to have the list separated onto individual cards (rather than keeping track of where you are on the list). This way, once a letter combination is used, that card can be moved to the back of the set, ensuring that it won't be repeated until students have had exposure to other letter combinations.

In the game, you will want to use letter combinations that are common in English. *Ch*, for example, both starts and ends many English words, so adding a vowel before or after *ch* will ensure that students have ready words in their minds. Of course, the greater challenge is to then separate the *c* from the *h*.

In Practice

An unexpected fire drill has once again hijacked the day's lesson. Students return to class with seven minutes left in the period. Not wanting to lose precious time, Paul asks his students to get out a piece of scrap paper. He writes *THE* on the chalkboard and tells the class (already intimately familiar with Wordsters) that they have two minutes. "GO!"

Students busily work to write words. Claire and Briana write the lists shown in Figures 4.1a and 4.1b.

THE

then
thane
other
calisthenics
writhe
another
authentic
rather
mother
father
brother
slather
slither
smother
thrive

THE

theatre
theme
theodore
theatrical
thematic
these
breathe
the
father
mother
brother
grandfather
them
mathematics
grandmother
their
they
together
other
feather

Figure 4.1a   *Wordster #1—Claire*   Figure 4.1b   *Wordster #1—Briana*

Paul calls time. The students stop writing and begin comparing their lists with their partners (although this can also be done in small groups). Notice that *mother*, *father*, *brother*, and *other* appear on both lists. So neither girl counts those words in her score. In this case, Claire scores eleven points and Briana scores sixteen points.

Next, Paul writes *SET* on the board and says, "GO!" Again, the class begins to write. After two additional minutes, Paul calls time, and students again compare their lists. Claire and Briana compare these lists in Figures 4.2a and 4.2b.

In this round, neither girl counts *reset*, but all of the others do count. Claire earns seven points and Briana earns eight. This example also shows how some letter combinations will prove more difficult. In the same amount of time, the girls generated a little better than half of the number in the previous round. Notice, too, that part of Briana's success with this letter combination was her knowledge of morphemes. Her list revolves around *SET* as a morpheme to which she added affixes, while Claire's list has more variety of words using the *SET* pattern.

SET

Set
Senate
senator
reset
onset
spinet
setting
street

Figure 4.2a *Wordster #2—Claire*

SET

setting
setter
reset
preset
upset
upsetting
asset
settle
settlement

Figure 4.2b *Wordster #2—Briana*

Differentiation

To make the game easier, use three-letter prefixes or suffixes that students are studying. This is likely to lead students to create a list of words that use the affix as a unit attached to a root. For example, if you write the letters *PRE*, students will likely produce a list with words like *predetermine*, *prefix*, *prelude*, and so forth. Although some students will stray from this pattern and add words like *practice* and *parachute* (unless you add a rule that they *must* use the letters as an affix to reinforce learned affixes), most will generate a word list that mimics their word study.

Instruction may be tailored to various students' needs when you have them play Wordsters in partnerships or small groups. This can be done in two ways. In one method, a pair or small group of students may compete against only each other, using the same rules as described earlier. Fewer students to compete against means students will generally be able to gain more points. Alternatively, each group can work together to compete against another group. In this situation, one student scribes while the rest brainstorm words, thus freeing some students to simply generate words rather than spell and write as well.

To make the game more challenging, add a rule stating that no letter in the sequence can be attached to another in the generated words. In this model, if the letter sequence is *SPA*, *space*, *special*, *especially* would not be accepted because some or all of the sequence is attached. *Superficial*, however, would work.

A Conversation with Kids

The Monday after the state tennis tournament, Laura and Kelly bounded into my classroom. I had heard that they had performed well at the tournament, and I was eager to congratulate them.

"Congratulations, girls. I heard you had a great weekend at the tennis match. Tell me about it!"

"Yeah, it was cool," Kelly began. "The drive was too long, though."

"I can imagine," I said, knowing that the tournament was a good four-hour drive from our town.

"You know what we did to pass the time?" Laura asked.

"What?"

"We played Wordsters," Laura responded.

"How did you manage that?"

"We used the letters from license plates. It was awesome," Laura said.

"Some of the letter combinations didn't work. Like, people have license plates like *QTX*. But it was still really cool," Kelly added.

"I hadn't thought about using license plates. What a great idea!" I beamed.

As I think about this conversation today, I still smile. Even armed with digital entertainment (radios, MP3 players, portable video games, etc.), these students elected to play a word game—because it was a challenge and because it was a fun way to interact with each other.

8-Count Rule

Playing word games like Wordsters provides a fun, challenging way to encourage students to access and practice with known words. However, the most important aspect of vocabulary acquisition and development is that students develop the ability to use powerful words in their own speech and writing. The 8-Count Rule directly teaches students to choose powerful and precise words when they write. When writing, students often use the first word that pops into their heads to describe something. Instead of allowing our students to settle for basic language, the 8-Count Rule helps teach them to search for the perfect word to convey meaning, making for powerful writing. Bringing word choice to the front of students' awareness makes for lasting improvements in their work.

Although loosely based on the analysis experts do to level text, the 8-Count Rule is a nonscientific method for approximating the reading level of a piece of writing. This strategy requires students to analyze the word choice in just eight sentences of text—either excerpts from the work of published authors or from students' own writing. After analyzing word choice through a series of steps (description follows), students count the high-powered (or precise) words in a series of eight sentences. This draws attention to the words students select when writing and encourages kids to become more precise with language. Studying what makes a piece of writing more sophisticated (and by proxy, more interesting) can help students to use the same tools in their own writing.

Optionally, students may correlate their word count to a leveling chart, but this isn't necessary and should be used thoughtfully.

Setup

Create an overhead transparency or PowerPoint slide with the following rules (or simply write them on a sheet of chart paper):

Count	Don't Count
multisyllabic words (3+ syllables)	proper nouns
◆ dynasty	one- and two-syllable words with a simple ending (-ing, -ed, -est, -er)
◆ everyone	
high-powered one- and two-syllable words	◆ beginning
	words used incorrectly
◆ abrupt	any word more than twice
◆ stealth	any word provided in the prompt
figurative language or words/phrases used in unique ways	
◆ employ my vision	

In Practice

Sharon's tenth-grade students are studying works by Edgar Allan Poe. Their writing assignment to emulate Poe's style to retell the story of Chicken Little challenges them to move beyond their comfort zones and use new, more interesting, more specific words in their writing. Before beginning that assignment, however, Sharon wants to stimulate students to become more aware of how using different vocabulary can change a piece of writing.

Using an excerpt from "The Pit and the Pendulum," Sharon puts the following on an overhead transparency:

> So far, I had not opened my eyes. I felt that I lay upon my back, unbound. I reached out my hand, and it fell heavily upon something damp and hard. There I suffered it to remain for many minutes, while I strove to imagine where and what I could be. I longed, yet dared not, to employ my vision. I dreaded the first glance at objects around me. It was not that I feared to look upon things horrible, but that I grew aghast lest there should be nothing to see. At length, with a wild desperation at heart, I quickly unclosed my eyes. My worst thoughts, then, were confirmed. The blackness of eternal night encompassed me. I struggled for breath. The intensity of the darkness seemed to oppress and stifle me. The atmosphere was intolerably close. I still lay quietly, and made effort to exercise my reason.

Sharon explains that these thirteen sentences come from the body of the short story, not the introduction or conclusion, so that they typify Poe's tone. She then reads the excerpt aloud to the class. After finishing, she says, "Today we are going to learn a vocabulary self-check strategy called the 8-Count. We will walk through the steps together and then you will be able to apply this strategy to your Chicken Little stories."

"First, we need to identify eight sentences to analyze. In an 8-Count, you don't want to use the introduction or conclusion unless you must, because those paragraphs often differ in language usage from the body of a text. So for our purposes today, we will consider the first and last sentences as the introduction and conclusion and ignore them. So I need to open brackets at the beginning of the second sentence, count eight sentences and close brackets after *confirmed*." She writes the brackets on the transparency and then puts up the 8-Count rules she has written on chart paper earlier.

> So far, I had not opened my eyes. [I felt that I lay upon my back, unbound. I reached out my hand, and it fell heavily upon something damp and hard. There I suffered it to remain for many minutes, while I strove to imagine where and what I could be. I longed, yet dared not, to employ my vision. I dreaded the first glance at objects around me. It was not that I feared to look upon things horrible, but that I grew aghast lest there should be nothing

to see. At length, with a wild desperation at heart, I quickly unclosed my eyes. My worst thoughts, then, were confirmed.] The blackness of eternal night encompassed me. I struggled for breath. The intensity of the darkness seemed to oppress and stifle me. The atmosphere was intolerably close. I still lay quietly, and made effort to exercise my reason.

"What we want to do now is to analyze the language usage of this piece of writing. The process we will use is similar to that of reading specialists who determine the difficulty of various books. Although we will not consider all of the traits that they do, this strategy will allow you to approximate the reading level of your own writing, so that you can all work to enhance it.

"Let's look at the 8-Count rules." Sharon reviews the guidelines with her students. "Okay, let's try counting this excerpt."

Sharon reads the first bracketed sentence aloud and asks if students see any words to count. *I felt that I lay upon my back, unbound.*

"None of those has three or more syllables, so none of them count," offers James.

"But who says *unbound*?" Alex challenges.

"No one," Kim says.

"What would an average person say?" Sharon asks, using this as a loose benchmark for high-powered one- and two-syllable words.

"Untied or free or something like that," Alex says.

"Okay, so if *unbound* isn't what the average person would say to indicate the same meaning, let's count it." Sharon highlights *unbound*. "What about the next sentence?"

"*Heavily* has three syllables," Jason says.

"Good." Sharon highlights *heavily*.

Together the class works through the eight sentences, highlighting all of the words that they determine should be "counted." Their collective 8-Count looks like this:

So far, I had not opened my eyes. [I felt that I lay upon my back, unbound. I reached out my hand, and it fell heavily upon something damp and hard. There I suffered it to remain for many minutes, while I strove to imagine where and what I could be. I longed, yet dared not, to employ my vision. I dreaded the first glance at objects around me. It was not that I feared to look upon things horrible, but that I grew aghast lest there should be nothing to see. At length, with a wild desperation at heart, I quickly unclosed my eyes. My worst thoughts, then, were confirmed.] The blackness of eternal night encompassed me. I struggled for breath. The intensity of the darkness seemed to oppress and stifle me. The atmosphere was intolerably close. I still lay quietly, and made effort to exercise my reason.

Counting the high-powered vocabulary, the students conclude that in the eight identified sentences, fourteen "count."

"So what does that mean?" Alex questions.

At this point, Sharon must make a decision about how to proceed. She could ask students to do a quick visual check for density of highlighted words. In this case, students will notice that Poe uses a considerable amount of precise and interesting language.

Or Sharon can choose to challenge students to think of the level of their vocabulary usage in terms of audience. If an author is penning a picture book, for example, basic and functional vocabulary is appropriate because the text is intended for elementary school children. On the other hand, if an author is writing a piece of research, technical language will likely increase the reading level. Because Sharon's students are working with a text none of them authored, and because she wants to encourage kids to keep audience in mind when writing, she opts for the latter.

"Well, let's look at a loose correlation. Zero to five counted words in eight sentences would be considered 'basic vocabulary.' While basic vocabulary is appropriate in many situations, how many of you want your academic writing to be viewed as basic? Six to ten counted words correlates to 'functional vocabulary'—like that in most newspaper articles. Eleven to fifteen counted words correlates to 'proficient vocabulary.' This would be appropriate for most academic work, particularly at high school level. And over sixteen counted words correlate to 'advanced vocabulary'—like academic research, technical text, and college textbooks."

"Wow. That's pretty cool," Jason offers.

Students then apply the 8-Count to eight sentences they have identified in their Chicken Little stories and work in pairs to discuss their findings. Some students are dismayed to learn that they counted fewer than five high-powered words in their own writing samples. As Sharon circulates around the room and notices this, she conferences with these students, saying, "I know you can increase your count because you know a lot of rich, wonderful words. When you revise, let's really focus on word choice and think about how each word affects your reader."

Sharon opens a class discussion by asking, "What factors do you think contribute to having a high count?"

"Well, you have to use good words," James says.

"But that's not enough," Jason counters. "You could have one great word in each sentence and still be in the functional range. You also have to have some long sentences so you have more words to choose from."

"And when you use figurative language, that counts," Alex adds.

"Good. So strong vocabulary, varied sentence structure, and imagery all help to increase your count—and also help make your writing a lot more interesting! Now I want you to work just on the eight sentences you identified in your own stories and revise those."

Review of the Steps

1. Identify eight sentences to count. Avoid introductions and conclusions if possible.
2. Count multisyllabic words, high-powered words, and figurative language in those eight sentences.
3. If desired, correlate the count to a "reading" level.

Author Reflection

Of the strategies I employed in my classroom, the 8-Count Rule was one of the most effective because it caused students to review their own writing through a specific lens. None of my students wanted to write with simply "functional" vocabulary. Initially, I challenged students to double their count if it was below eight. While this activity exposed their errant thesaurus skills, it did lead me to develop another strategy—The Power of the Incomprehensible Essay, described in the next section.

Ultimately, students became comfortable automatically doing an 8-Count on excerpts from each piece of writing that they took through the writing process to publication—and they checked their work at multiple points throughout the piece to ensure consistency with readability, thus reinforcing that authors write for an audience. As students became more adept at accessing the rich words in their minds, we worked on stylistic techniques to vary readability for impact. Time and time again, students commented that this strategy helped them to seek out the best word to convey their intended meaning rather than settling for just any word that would fit.

Differentiation

With struggling writers, the use of published text rather than their own writing removes personalization, allowing them to truly analyze an excerpt of text for word choice. When using published works, be certain to vary the excerpts in readability, purpose, and style to keep the strategy interesting and to encourage discussion.

The benefit of using published material should be noted for all students. Exemplars will push even the most capable of writers to pull words out of their lexicons, digging for the best fit.

The Power of the Incomprehensible Essay

Students' first attempts to revise their stories after the 8-Count activity immediately exposed their lack of experience using a thesaurus. These sophomores believed that to up the reading level of their writing, they should grab a thesaurus, look up any dull word, and replace that dull word with some multisyllabic "synonym." Never mind that they didn't have any clue what the synonyms really meant—their nuances, their connotations, their relative strength compared to other listed words. In these kids' world, all synonyms were created equal. The result, as you can imagine, was a collection of incomprehensible work.

Unlike other strategies described in this text, The Power of the Incomprehensible Essay works only once a year. That said, kids love the challenge, and the essays are a great deal of fun. The idea came to me after watching an episode of the sitcom *Friends*. In one particular episode, the characters Chandler and Monica are beginning the adoption process and ask their well-intentioned but perpetually confused friend Joey to write a letter of recommendation to their caseworker. Even Joey's best effort sounded juvenile. In fact, the caseworker called Chandler to say how sweet it was that they asked a child to write one of their letters but that the agency wouldn't be able to use it. Surprised, he asked which child and was shocked to hear that it was Joey.

When Chandler confronted Joey about the letter, he asked, "Haven't you ever heard of a thesaurus?" Joey, not surprisingly, had not. In a brief, simplified introduction to this resource, Chandler explained that you can use a thesaurus to look up any word and find a better word. But Chandler's explanation was too basic: Joey rewrote his letter replacing practically every word, making it completely incomprehensible (and very funny!).

I wondered, could students take a poorly written or very basic essay and instead of making improvements, make it incomprehensible? What a challenge! To do that, they would be forced to consider the nuances of words and deliberately select the wrong ones.

Setup

First, make sure that you have taught your students the 8-Count Rule before using this strategy. Students must understand how to approximate a reading level.

Next, write up a short piece needing significant vocabulary improvement to use as an example. The meaning, however, can be relatively simple. Although the strategy is called the Incomprehensible *Essay*, the piece can take any form. Letters tend to work well because they give students a clear sense of audience when they write. Finally, ensure that each student has access to a thesaurus and a dictionary.

When I use this strategy, I try to adapt my writing to a form students are studying. I also work to keep the writing rather open, rather than conveying any specific meaning. An example might look like this:

Dear Susan,

The beach is nice. We are lucky that the weather has been good—no rain! I think we are all getting a nice tan, but the sand is too hot. The water is nice, but, as you know, I'm afraid to swim in the ocean.

Yesterday we played beach volleyball with some kids from Florida. They were really good. Of course, they probably live on the beach and play all of the time.

I'm sad that you broke your leg and aren't able to be here. Everyone says hi.

Friends,

Colleen

In Practice

Share your example essay or letter with your students. Apply the 8-Count Rule to an excerpt from your essay (make sure that you've done this yourself already so you know what to expect). Ask students how they might change the piece to make it better. Then challenge students to change the essay's meaning *entirely* simply by changing the low-level words into high-level words (see Figure 4.3). If students' ages make showing the *Friends* episode appropriate, show the portions related to the task at hand.

Sample

Prized Susan,

Being stranded is quaint. We are believed to bring good fortune and the storm systems are excellent. In total we are being paid a kind coffee, but the grain is most outrageous. The tears are also kind, but, I'm still terrified to bathe in the deep.

In former times, we tricked stranded sports with cretins hailing from Florida. They were most superior. Alas, they are denizens of the stranded and trick sports in every occasion.

It is poignant that you lack means with your appendage and don't exist at this juncture. All persons dictate greetings.

Acquaintances,

Colleen

Figure 4.3 *Incomprehensible Essay*

Cascade Poems

Most people's brains jump into a different gear when writing poetry. The task itself seems to demand eloquence and precision. When you add to the challenge of writing a poem the restriction to not only use specific words but use them in a specific *order*, as is the case with cascade poems, you challenge students to play with high-level vocabulary and to discover relationships among seemingly unrelated words.

Setup

Because cascade poems really challenge kids' thinking, you will want to be thoughtful when selecting the number of words (which also dictates the number of lines) to use. Students' first response to this activity is a gasp, followed by the belief they will *never* be able to write a cascade poem. Be strong and tell them to take heart. These poems are generally amazingly powerful.

After determining how many words/lines will be included (start small!), ask various students to give you a list of words—either random words or words related to a topic you have studied. Write the words on the chalkboard, numbering them as they are listed. After reaching your desired number of words, stop.

Explain to students that they will be writing a poem in which the words will cascade, or tumble, down the poem. The first word on the list should appear as the first word in the first line of the poem. The second word as the second word in the second line of the poem, and so on.

In Practice

Victoria asked her students to generate a list of high-powered words—one per line of the poem to be written. Although the following samples use twelve words and lead to twelve-line poems, start with lists of six to eight words when introducing this strategy. She wrote the words on the chalkboard in the order students provided them.

In class, students generated this list:

1. teacher
2. music
3. comprehend
4. fluid

5. essence
6. resonate
7. home
8. secret
9. pursue
10. character
11. virtual
12. rendition

Victoria then explained that the students would each write a poem adhering to these guidelines: The words must be used in order; word one should be the first word in the first line of the poem, word two the second word in the second line of the poem, and so on (thus, cascading down the poem); students may elect to make one change in either word or placement in the line.

On the chalkboard, Victoria drew a chart indicating where the listed words should be (see below). She suggested to students that they make a similar chart to ensure proper placement of the words.

teacher									
	music								
		comprehend							
			fluid						
				essence					
					resonate				
						home			
							secret		
									etc.

Students were encouraged to write about any topic, but they had to find a coherent relationship among the words. Because the poem would be considerable in length and challenge students' thinking, Victoria gave students the option of working in pairs, allowing them time in class to work on their poems. Victoria was astounded by the variation in the students' poems, all resulting from the same twelve words! Jennifer's poem differs significantly from Maria's. Jennifer's poem reads:

Arise!
Today music abounds and creation
Called to comprehend—not merely understand the movement but
To experience the fluid crescendos and decrescendos
Bounding arpeggios demonstrate the essence of life
Each note created to truly resonate with the spirit
To rise and fall, to find home
Arise! The beauty of life is no secret
Nothing voiceless. The music calls us to seek, pursue, and find
To move in symphony with others while maintaining individual character
Arise! The music expresses honest, deep identity, nothing feigned, nothing virtual,
     only the real expression
Of each life living in community. No translation, no performance, no rendition. One
     grand symphony. Arise!

In contrast, see Maria's poem (Figure 4.4).

cascade in two

teacher; my father
his music; his love
he can't comprehend;
doesn't understand this fluid dance of relationships
labeled necessities of human essence; indispensable
anguish, torment, paranoia seem to resonate within him
he has a house; but no home to speak of
in his basement lives a threatening family secret; a monster
my stomach becomes unsettled at the desire to pursue this beast
my nightmares, my creations, will always hold this morphing character
I treasure the kiss of another world, my home of virtual reality
it is only here that my father, my monster, my beast rendition slumbers;
it is my safety

Figure 4.4 *Cascade Poem*

Both poems demonstrate the students' unique ideas and ability to connect seemingly random words. So often these poems relate to what the writer is experiencing on any given day. In the fall of 1994, I wrote about Colorado wildfires that I had experienced when visiting home during the summer. I recalled the ash falling like snow, even in the suburbs of Denver. But my Georgia students wrote about the floods they had experienced that same summer, the start of a new school year, and music and entertainment interesting to teenagers. On a different day, those same random words will provoke a different poem, even from the same poet.

Weighty Words

Weighty Words, a writing activity that challenges students to think outside the box about words, was adapted from *The Weighty Word Book* (Levitt et al. 2000). This ingenious alphabet book includes twenty-six words, each with a story playing on the word's sound to express its meaning. In this activity, students use a play on a word's sound to write a story that will help the reader vividly remember its definition—for example, the word *yeoman* might be translated, using its sound, into the phrase *Yo! Men!* The resulting story, based around the word's true *meaning*, could be about getting the attention of a group of fellows guarding something.

Setup

Ideally, teachers would secure a copy of *The Weighty Word Book* to use as an example for students. Students will also need one of the two word graphic organizers shown below, and a dictionary. The simpler of the graphic organizers, a Frayer Model (see diagram on the next page), will capture all of the needed information.

Alternatively, teachers could opt for a more complex organizer that captures additional information (see Figure 4.5 on page 80).

Write multisyllabic words on slips of paper and put them in a hat. For ideas, see Appendix C. Be certain to avoid those words included in the alphabet book. Although students don't typically plagiarize these stories, I

Definition:	Example:
My own association:	Nonexample:

have found that once a story idea for a word is in the mind, it's difficult to invent something different.

In Practice

Read the chosen selection from *The Weighty Word Book*. (My personal favorite is *expedient*.) If necessary, review syllabication.

Have each student draw one of the words from the hat. If a student does not like his word, he may change it, but he must find an alternate word and gain teacher approval for it. Because my students made a class alphabet book using the stories resulting from their words, I required that the new word start with the same letter as the rejected word. No words may be those from *The Weighty Word Book*.

Students complete the graphic organizer for the word they have chosen. Then they brainstorm plays on the word's sound that they will later use to create a story. In the story, the student must use the broken syllables of the word to create an association, so just repeating the word several times will give kids a sense of the sounds they have to work with.

Vocabulary Graphic Organizer

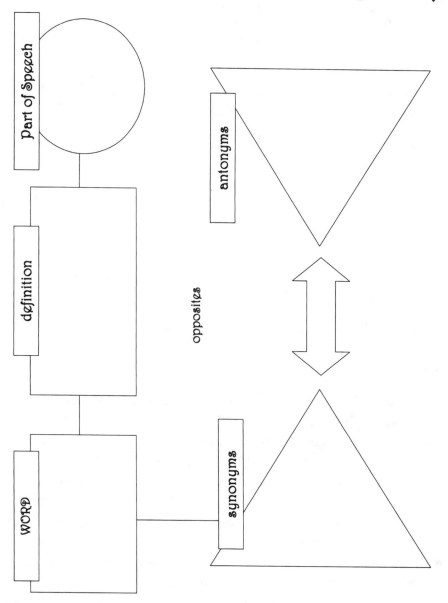

Figure 4.5   *Vocabulary Graphic Organizer*

May be copied for classroom use. © 2008 by Sandra R. Whitaker, from *Word Play* (Heinemann: Portsmouth, NH).

The primary focus of the story should be to define the vocabulary word through storytelling. So, when kids are working with the syllables, it is important for them to think about what other words they know that sound similar. *Malleable*, for example, includes *able*, so something that is *malleable* is *able* to bend. *Insipid*, on the other hand, sounds like *sip it*. So a story around this word might include a character who slurps her tea instead of sipping it, making her lacking in tasteful characteristics. Depending on your publication goals, students may also draw a picture for inclusion in a final class project.

As students prepare to revise and publish their stories, Paul works on a detailed drawing of a shattered *F*. This will accompany his story for the word *fragmented*. Gina draws a girl doing gymnastics. Her images almost create the motion as the character reshapes her body to flip across a balance beam. This will accompany her story for the word *malleable*.

Although the Weighty Word activity will be completed only once, each student will receive a copy of the alphabet book. Throughout the semester, they will reread various stories and discuss the words' meanings and morphemic structure. In the spring, each student will be accountable in class presentations and through their writing for the words in the three classes' collaborative alphabet book.

STEP INTO A CLASSROOM

The heat of August permeates the classroom at C and Main. Dictionaries scattered about, students work in writing groups to share and revise their word stories. Across three sophomore classes, the word stories will be compiled into an alphabet book that will become a portion of the students' vocabulary work for the semester.

Monica's story about a *camel's lodge* captivates her group. She describes a distant land where pharaohs rule and a simple life isn't so simple. Her hero works to hide his family's only valuable possession, a camel, from the soldiers raiding their town. Her word? *Camouflage*.

Simultaneously, Kevin tells the story of Austin, a teen with a brand-new sports car—red, convertible, the works. Of course, everyone he knows wants a ride. Everyone screams, "*Austin, take us!*" The word? *Ostentatious*.

Kristen reads her story (Figure 4.6) to the writing group.

Deep in the heart of the forest, nothing stirred but the singing of the fireflies. They each sung their own tune. Although they sang during the night, during the day they buzzed busily with their own business. One day, news spread round the colony of the beautiful words of Mono Shakespeare, the firefly writer of the century. When anyone read his stories, they were swept away into lands far away. Everyone who read Mono's stories would float away happily.

The whole firefly colony was happy, except for one firefly. Although Mono could create the richest writing, he was not happy. He did not like being a writer, he wanted to sing.

He kept this a secret for years upon years, as he practiced with his voice by himself.

All the fireflies were filled with eagerness. It was the beginning of spring, and Mono was going to have his author's reception in the middle of May.

Everyone was eager for the reception, except Mono. Although he wrote all his lines for the reception, beautiful to say the least, there was an empty space inside. Again that night he warmed up his voice. La.... La... La...La..., when his head was hit with an original idea. I could sing for my authors reception. He added music to all his lines and started to practice.

In the blink of an eye, it was the day of the reception, and all the fireflies arrived early at the reception hall. Soon everyone was there, including the mayor, but no Mono.

The doors opened, and down the floor a dancing, twirling Mono sang. He sang his lines, but he was struck by sadness when he heard the sounds of snoring.

He turned around with tears flowing from his eyes. Mayor... Mayor...! What did I do wrong? The mayor's reply was simple and quick, "Your words were still beautiful, but you made no emphasis and it was the same repeated tone."

So when you hear somebody that makes you fall asleep, think of Mono and his repeated tone and you will remember.

Monotonous

Figure 4.6 *Weighty Word—Monotonous*

Differentiation

Although this activity may seem too difficult for middle school students, it isn't! In fact, fifth-grade students have risen to the challenge and compiled an amazing alphabet book for their class. A little persistence and differentiation are the key.

Exemplars, either from *The Weighty Word Book* or from students, will help to clarify the play on words. Working with known puns (*That's hot!* meaning both temperature and interest) will also help students to visualize plays on sound and meaning.

Selecting words within students' reach is crucial for success. Many multisyllabic and interesting words are within middle school students' ability to manipulate and extend into a story. Alternatively, you may choose monosyllabic homonyms that have proven confusing to your students. Stories around these words help students to associate the homonyms and to recall stories to distinguish them. This student story for *feat* (Figure 4.7) is one example.

Why? Why? Why? Was all you would hear "big feet Joe" say. He always said Why, Why, Why, because he had the biggest feet anyone had *ever* seen! They were seriously enormous. He was 5 feet tall and wore a size 20 shoes. Depression and his *huge feet* was what Joe was known for. He was always depressed because, when he was little (before he got big feet) he had a dream to play some sport in the summer Olympics. ANY SPORT! He thought that his dream could never come true because he had such big feet.

One Christmas Eve night, since Joe was Christian he decided to pray to God and tell Him everything he was thinking. He prayed and prayed and prayed. He told God *everything* about his life, his big feet, his depression, and, of course his lifelong dream about the Olympics.

That night Joe had a dream about the Summer Olympics. He dreamed about all of the events they had, mostly the long jump though. When Joe awoke the next morning he knew the dream was a sign . God had given the dream to Joe. Joe thought god was absolutely brilliant and he decided he was going to go if not try to go to the Olympics.

On Christmas morning Joe went into his backyard and practiced jumping. He was actually really good. His huge feet *actually* helped him get higher and longer elevation. Joe put sand in his backyard a couple of days later and lines to measure how far he could jump.

For four months everyday he would practice. Everyday he would go further than the day before. That summer what do you know, he competed in the long jump event at the Summer Olympics! He had practiced *so much* and had *so much* determination he won!

If you ever doubt yourself remember Joe and his big...

Feat

Figure 4.7   *Weighty Word*—Feat

In Summary

Much of vocabulary instruction is about activating students' word knowledge by creating situations in which using high-powered vocabulary becomes the normal expectation. These activities also allow students to take words from their reading and gain control over their use in other contexts. Rather than relying on receptive vocabulary being adequate for success, students are challenged to move new words into their productive vocabulary and to incorporate those words into their speaking and writing.

SECTION *TWO*

Conceptual Meaning Makers

Understanding: Readers must own specific words to understand the text at hand.

Thirty-seven sophomores spill into the library ready to begin their research projects. In class they have discussed the parameters of the project and possible topics, which must relate to the Harlem Renaissance. While some students go directly to the stacks and others begin queries on the electronic catalog, Sam and Anthony want to maximize the use of electronic resources.

Unsure of how to use the numerous databases to which the school subscribes, Sam looks at Anthony and says, "What should we do first?"

"I don't remember all that stuff Ms. Kelsey showed us at the beginning of the year. Let's just Google it."

Why and How to Teach Conceptual Meaning Makers

5

Google the phrase "conceptual meaning makers," and you will find nothing. Trust me, I tried it. But Google doesn't know everything—yet. So just what are conceptual meaning makers? And if Google doesn't know about them, why are they so important?

Nagy and Anderson (1984) determined that a mere 5,000 words account for 95 percent of all running text. In other words, a *really small* number of words accounts for *almost all* of the text students encounter in their school years. Moreover, when you consider that my three-year-old already knows a couple thousand of those words, and that the average kindergartner starts school knowing nearly all of those words, you see that most of running text is relatively basic. That said, why does text often perplex so many readers?

Although basic vocabulary—words like *is*, *her*, *do*—comprises the majority of the words on the average page (95 percent, to be precise), the other five percent of words tend to carry the meaning. Of that other 5 percent, some words' conceptual meaning will be applicable to a wide range of texts, but other words' meaning may be narrower in scope and less relevant. For that reason, teachers should focus on pre-teaching and emphasizing those words that make meaning for a wide range of text—the conceptual meaning makers.

An example of a conceptual meaning maker might be the word *representation*. In a U.S. history class, this word will appear in many texts.

Therefore, teachers should ensure that students start with a solid understanding on which they can continue to build, adding examples each time the word is encountered in a new context.

Conversely, the word *dowager*, while an interesting word, may appear in only one short story that the students will read in the entire school year—or even over several years. In this instance, consider highlighting other, more transferable words in the text, and when students come across the word *dowager*, simply *tell* them that a dowager is an elderly, widowed woman holding property from her late husband and move on.

Sometimes determining the most important words to highlight can be tricky business. We can never be certain exactly which words each of our students already knows, so this process becomes largely a guessing game. That said, we can never go wrong teaching, or reinforcing, those words that students will encounter repeatedly in a variety of contexts. Each time a word is heard, it's brought back to the front of the mind, automatically nudging students to reconsider its use.

Building conceptual understanding with kids requires teaching them how to think in both broad and specific ways. They must understand words' specific uses, but they also must be able to classify, store, and access them from a variety of conceptual files or compartments.

I like to think of these overarching concepts as containers, like big paint buckets, that information pours into. As kids learn new information, our job as experts in our disciplines is to help kids link that information to overarching concepts. This knowledge helps students to use a variety of resources to apply strategies to new situations across disciplines. If students recognize the traits of something (like morphemic structure) as being related to a larger concept (like systems) and thus to another topic within that larger concept (like an ecosystem), they will be able to approach learning that new information through a particular lens (or multiple lenses), thus deepening their understanding. In this case, knowing that ecosystems require balance and follow predictable patterns will help students understand the predictable patterns of language.

Likewise, figurative language and syntax are largely matters of aesthetics. Without them, writing could follow a precise formula and all writing would sound the same. But these nuances of author's craft make each piece unique. When students connect these aspects of writing to art, for example, they see that figurative language and syntax help make the masterpiece rather than paint by numbers.

Building Concepts

Since she was five, my eight-year-old daughter and I have played the "concept game" when riding in the car. The idea is simple: One of us states a category and then we take turns providing examples of things that fit into that category. A basic exchange for "things that live in the ocean" might include *dolphins, coral, whales, turtles,* and the like. In this instance, I might toss in something like *submarine* to add new vocabulary or to get beyond the living things she naturally envisions. The next category might be "mammals," in which *whales* and *dolphins* will also appear, leading her to think about the traits of mammals versus the traits of fish. In more complex interpretations of a category, say "things that fly," we go beyond literal meanings to figurative meanings—including *birds, airplanes, flags,* and *tempers.* Each of these exchanges challenges us to think about common objects and ideas in new ways.

In classrooms, we should play similar games with students, thus challenging them to rethink the attributes of learned content knowledge and vocabulary. Although we could simply play this same concept game, making up our own rules, years ago I happened upon Perpetual Notion, a game that accomplishes the same goal and is easily adapted for classroom use.

Perpetual Notion

Perpetual Notion, based on the Pressman Toy Corporation board game, is a variation on the basic "concept game" that I play with my children. It requires students to discover and create conceptual links between words. Although the board game is played with a series of word cards that players draw and play in connection to previously played cards, students can play in class with word cards they've already made as part of a particular unit of study—thus requiring little setup beyond explaining the rules of play. The game works well with social studies, science, English, and even mathematics units.

Setup

Often, throughout a unit of study, students work in groups to create word cards (I use index cards) with new vocabulary words and other topically relevant words. For example, a history class may be studying the foundations of our nation. Students' word cards might include these terms: *taxation, war, representation, crown, Great Britain, Loyalist, traitor, Williamsburg, Boston, weapon, Colonist, Virginia,* and so on. If these cards have not been made throughout the unit, it's not hard to have students make them on the fly before introducing the game.

In small groups, students shuffle the cards and distribute between three and five cards to each player. The remaining cards are placed in a central stack. Thinking of a concept that relates to the unit at hand, the first player places a card face up in front of him and draws a card from the stack. In this move, the student might place the word *Williamsburg* in front of him, thinking about the capital of Virginia during the Revolutionary War. The player to his right then places one of her cards face up. These two cards must have a conceptual link. The second student need not be thinking of precisely the same concept as the first student—she must simply be able to justify her thinking if challenged. For instance, she could play *sentinel,* thinking of the people who may have lived in Williamsburg at the time. Or, if thinking along the same lines as the first player, she could play *Richmond,* which became the capital of Virginia in 1780. Going around in a circle, students take turns placing cards on the table and drawing from the stack. Each word card played must have a conceptual link to all of the other cards. Throughout the course of the game, the concept will undoubtedly evolve, thus challenging students to think flexibly about concepts associated with the unit and deepen their understanding.

If a group member believes that a played card does not work to describe a concept in his thinking, he can challenge the student who played the card. To do this, the challenged student must state the concept he was thinking of and then explain how each played word fits. If no player is called on to explain a concept during play, the final student to play a card must explain the concept and how the words relate.

Generally, students challenge each other before random cards are played in an attempt to simply keep the game going. If a challenged player cannot explain a logical connection, she removes her card and forfeits her turn. Of course, these events present teaching moments, during which peers—or you, as the teacher—can intervene and correct misconceptions.

STEP INTO A CLASSROOM

Joanie, a middle school history teacher, has been working with her seventh-grade students to help them understand the complexities of the American Revolution. Joanie's goals for her students include knowing the key people (and their contributions) during the American Revolution, the causes and results of the war, and the principles on which our nation was founded. She decides to challenge and assess students' conceptual knowledge of this time period by playing Perpetual Notion.

In the backpack-littered classroom, the students have rearranged their desks into "tables" and are sitting in groups of four. In addition to their student-created cards for Perpetual Notion, Joanie has created a set of stock cards with basic nouns and verbs. These don't necessarily tie directly to the unit vocabulary but add cards that help students to connect vocabulary from the unit to everyday descriptions, like *magnetic*. For a science unit, this may relate to a specific and literal magnetic field or attraction, but in the more general sense, it could relate to items being drawn to one another. These are on pink index cards while the kids' cards are white, making the stock cards easy to identify for sorting later. Students have already shuffled these stock cards into their stacks and are beginning play.

Joanie moves through the room, listening in on group discussions and facilitating the game. She stops to observe one group and sees that the following cards have been placed on the table: *taxation, Declaration of Independence, Virginia, treason, representation, Burgesses.* At this point, Carol, an outgoing redhead, says, "Okay, Susan, explain that. How does *Burgesses* go with the *Declaration of Independence?*"

(Continued)

Taking a deep breath, Susan begins, "Thomas Jefferson. He didn't believe in taxation without representation, one of the causes of the American Revolution. He was from Virginia and served in the House of Burgesses there, in Williamsburg. And he signed the Declaration of Independence, and committed treason in doing so—and in participating in the war. There."

Impressed with the linkage but curious about one omitted detail, Joanie asks, "What was Jefferson's role in the scripting and signing of the Declaration of Independence?"

"He wrote it," Ashley responds knowingly.

"*And* he signed it," Susan says.

"Yes, he did both. Well done."

Joanie moves on to another group. This group has come across some of the stock cards. The played cards include: *freedom, tyranny, taxation, boat, winter, Boston, tea*. In this case, the outcome seems fairly logical, but Joanie asks Marcella to explain the event to which the cards point to make sure that they are on track.

"Well, it's the Boston Tea Party. The colonists were tired of being taxed by Great Britain. They thought the king was a tyrant. They had moved to the colonies for freedom, but with all the British soldiers living there with them, there wasn't much of that. They were still bound by British rules. So in December of 1773, three boats docked in Boston Harbor, and the colonists dumped all of the goods overboard."

"Okay, so let's go back and talk about what each person was thinking as the cards were played."

"Well, I figured *freedom* was about the most open card I could play because it relates to everything about the American Revolution, so I played that first," Sydney, a rather shy girl says.

"Then I added *tyranny* because I was thinking of the British crown. The colonists wanted freedom from the crown," Marcella adds.

"*Taxation* was one of the reasons the colonists were so angry," Desmond explains, tugging at the strings on his sweatshirt hood.

"I played *boat* thinking about the start of the war and Paul Revere's ride," Calliope jumps in. "I thought I might trick someone, but I didn't."

"No, because I added *winter* thinking of the Boston Tea Party," Sydney says.

"Would Paul Revere's Ride still have worked?" Joanie asks.

"No. That was in April, so *winter* spoils that," Desmond volunteers.

"Excellent." Joanie smiles and heads toward another group, trying not to trip over the backpacks.

Differentiation

The more closely related the cards kids start out with, the simpler the game, because the connections between them will be more obvious from the beginning. Arguably, in the previous example, students could have said the American Revolution in general was the concept for every game, so the teacher can set some boundaries—like thinking of specific events, people, or places—before kids play to encourage more specific conceptual solutions.

In Joanie's case, she chose to add some stock cards to students' sets, which made the game both more authentic and more difficult. Because not all of the words necessarily relate to the unit at hand, students may encounter a situation in which only one of their cards will make sense, forcing them to make a connection they may not have seen otherwise. To challenge students further, allow the card sets to build throughout the year instead of using unit-specific sets. When students are asked to make conceptual connections between words that relate to different units of study, they

---

STEP INTO A CLASSROOM

It is spring, and Joanie's students are now working on connecting concepts across the year's units of study. Playing Perpetual Notion has become extremely challenging as the game cards now number over 100 for each group. As the year has progressed, the game concepts have broadened, challenging students to make connections across different time periods and historical situations.

Joanie stops to look at one group's played cards. They include: *pilgrims, Thanksgiving, Jamestown, struggle, allied forces.* Sydney calls Marcella on her play.

"Well, it seemed pretty boring with everything pointing toward the early struggles of the pilgrims and colonists. So here's how I see it. The concept is cooperation. The pilgrims and Native Americans had to cooperate or the pilgrims would have died. That's the whole Thanksgiving thing: cooperation. Jamestown is an example of cooperation, too. They all had to work together to build the original fort and to survive. But that's also the goal of allied forces, to cooperate in the midst of a struggle or conflict."

Ultimately, this type of conversation among kids allows them to challenge their own thinking and to make connections between ideas. In short, they are playing the concept game without naming the general topic or unit of study to related concepts first. Gaining that depth of conceptual knowledge, though, requires multiple opportunities to play the game throughout the year.

must think more deeply not only about the specifics of each unit but also about larger concepts that might apply to many units' content.

Probable Passage

Traditionally designed to help students make predictions about fictional text, this strategy, which is easily adapted for nonfiction text, front-loads key vocabulary. By asking students to use key vocabulary to predict a passage's overall meaning and generate questions to be answered when reading, they are estimating its probable content. Because the original strategy and the adaptations are equally valuable, this section will introduce three ways to set up the strategy and explain how to use each method with kids.

Setup

Original Probable Passage

In the original strategy (Wood 1984), while planning for instruction, the teacher reads a passage new to students and selects ten to fifteen key words from the passage to highlight and pre-teach. Using those words, the teacher prepares a summary that uses those words and deletes the words from the summary, leaving blanks in their place.

During class, the teacher and students read through the list of deleted words and discuss them, ensuring that all students understand their meaning. Then the class charts the words into categories such as character, setting, actions, conflicts, and objects. Then students work to place words in the teacher-created summary. To accomplish this task, students must think about the words' definitions and what they know about story structure to predict placement of the words in the summary.

Adapted Probable Passage

Kylene Beers (2003) adapted this strategy, combining it with GIST (Generating Interactions between Schemata and Text) statements, thus challenging students to make a prediction statement about the passage based on key vocabulary. In this adaptation, the teacher again reads a passage and determines key vocabulary necessary for understanding that passage. After learning the words, students categorize them in boxes for characters, setting, problem, outcomes, unknown words, and to discover (or questions I have). Although this can be accomplished as a class, students can record the class-generated information on a graphic organizer. Alternatively, students can use that organizer to generate their own predictions first, before class discussion. Students then use those classifications to write their own GIST statement, thus predicting the passage's meaning and setting a purpose for reading.

For this particular assignment, the teacher provided her sixth-grade students with the following list of words to sort into categories: 1781, farm in Virginia, Jack Jouett, neglected, Cuckoo Tavern, full moon, Tarleton's Raider, no government, Thomas Jefferson, Patrick Henry, forty miles, Monticello, warned most of the legislators, slipped away, sword missing. Quamisha sorted the words and wrote her GIST statement (see Figure 5.1).

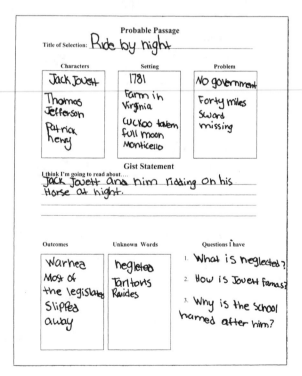

Figure 5.1 *Probable Passage—Jack Jouett*

After reading, students reviewed their initial Probable Passage and made corrections, if necessary (see Figure 5.2).

Nonfiction Probable Passage

Both of these versions front-load vocabulary and set a purpose for reading, thus engaging kids in a text before they begin to read. In response to the range of students' background knowledge, in our school system, we adapted the strategy again to include conceptual words related to the text. In this adaptation, the teacher selects the conceptual meaning makers in the text (not just the unknown or potentially difficult words) and words related to the text that may not appear in the text itself. Again, kids learn and sort the words. In this case, I use these categories: context/setting, characters/people, problem, causes and effects, solution, and questions I

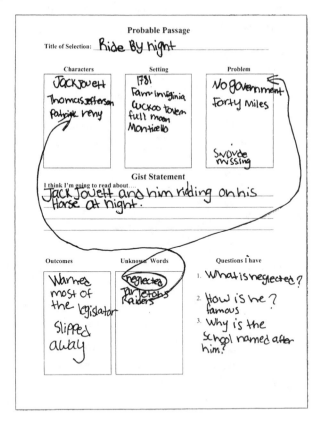

Figure 5.2 *Probable Passage—Jack Jouett (corrected)*

think the text will answer. In this adaptation, kids may also write a prediction statement about the text.

Recently, I was working with middle school students in social studies classes. The classroom teacher asked them to read a story about the Triangle Shirtwaist Factory fire. Certainly there are conceptual words in the text—*immigrant, union,* and *working conditions,* to name a few—but some key words to help students put the story in historical context do not appear in the article—*industrialization, sweatshop,* and *protest.* These added words provide additional context, giving students cues to the setting and key outcome of the event depicted in the story.

Working with words from the text and a few key related words helps students not only to learn difficult words in the text and use them to make predictions about meaning but will help kids to contextualize the text before reading.

In this example, eighth-grade students are preparing to read an article about the military. After completing their Probable Passage, the teacher reviewed key terminology and students took notes (see Figures 5.3a and 5.3b).

Name: Taylor   Teacher: Mr Sansing   Class Periods: 2nd   Date:

"The Military Get Mightier" Probable Passage

Directions: Categorize the key, clue words below by speculating where each word belongs in the graphic organizer. In the last space provided on the organizer, use your work with these words to predict what the article will be about. As we read the text, you will be able to come back to your prediction and to revise it based on what you've read.

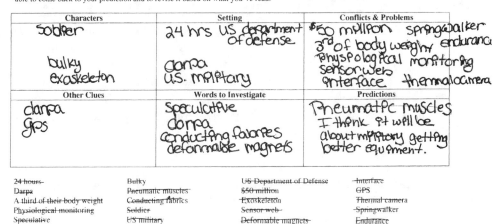

Characters	Setting	Conflicts & Problems
soldier	24 hrs US department of defense	$50 million springwalker
		3rd of body weight endurance
bulky		physiological monitoring
exoskeleton	darpa	sensor web
	U.S. military	interface thermalcamera

Other Clues	Words to Investigate	Predictions
darpa	speculative	Pneumatic muscles
gps	darpa	I think it will be
	conducting fabrics	about military getting
	deformable magnets	better equipment.

24 hours
Darpa
A third of their body weight
Physiological monitoring
Speculative

Bulky
Pneumatic muscles
Conducting fabrics
Soldier
US military

US Department of Defense
$50 million
Exoskeleton
Sensor web
Deformable magnets

Interface
GPS
Thermal camera
Springwalker
Endurance

Figure 5.3a   *Beers Probable Passage—Military*

darpa- research project for meliptary stuff

Conducting fabrics - fabric that carries electricity
safety

Physiological monitoring - monitoring year life signs

Speculative - going forward / a set answer.
Predicting

interface - controls for something

Pneumatic muscles - air pressure muscle

deformable magnets - magnets that can
change shape, but still work

Figure 5.3b   *Beers Probable Passage—Military*

STEP INTO A LANGUAGE ARTS CLASSROOM

The eighth-grade students in Brad's language arts class are preparing to read *The Diary of Anne Frank*, a stage play adapted from the well-known diary. To help students better understand that the play is a somewhat fictionalized account of a real event that involved real people, Brad and his students are reading an excerpt from *Anne Frank Remembered* by Miep Geis (and Alison Gold) (1988), one of the individuals who helped to hide the Frank family during the Holocaust. The excerpt reads:

More than twenty thousand Dutch people helped to hide Jews and others in need of hiding during those years. I willingly did what I could to help. My husband did as well. It was not enough.

There is nothing special about me. I have never wanted special attention. I was only willing to do what was asked of me and what seemed necessary at the time. When I was persuaded to tell my story, I had to think of the place that Anne Frank holds on history and what her story has come to mean for the many millions of people who have been touched by it. I'm told that every night when the sun goes down, somewhere in the world the curtain is going up on the stage play made from Anne's diary . . . her voice has reached the far edges of the earth. . . .

In some instances, more than fifty years have passed, and many details of events recorded in this book are half-forgotten. I have reconstituted conversations and events as closely as possible to the way I remember them. It is not easy to recall these memories in such detail. Even with the passing of time, it does not get easier.

My story is a story of very ordinary people during extraordinary terrible times. Times the like of which I hope with all my heart will never, never come again. It is for all of us ordinary people all over the world to see to it that they do not.

Because the passage does not include some of the key conceptual vocabulary that students will need to understand both this reading and the play, Brad has decided to use an Adapted Probable Passage to teach these conceptual meaning makers. In addition to key words that appear in the text, he adds words related to the text that will help students make more accurate predications and will front-load key concepts the students will encounter throughout their study. The word/phrase list he prepares for students is: *Dutch, Jews, tyranny, betrayal, ordinary people, extraordinary times, oppression, liberation, to go into hiding, protector, conceal, concentration camp, innocence, Nazi, Auschwitz, Bergen-Belsen, anti-Semitism, Holocaust, holocaust, gratitude, invasion.* Brad puts the list of words on the chalkboard as students arrive in class.

"You wrote *Holocaust* twice, Mr. Wheeler," McKenzie says knowingly.

"Did I? Well, let's see if there's a reason for that." Brad asks students to get out a sheet of paper and, with a partner, brainstorm what they think they already know about the words on the board. As students complete this task, Brad attends to taking roll and then circulates around the room. After a few minutes, he says, "In preparation for reading *The Diary of Anne Frank*, I thought it might be helpful to learn some key vocabulary that we will encounter. Let's review the words on the board." Brad reads the words, asking for students' ideas about them and clarifying definitions. When the class gets to the *Holocaust, holocaust* portion of the list, Brad is curious to see how students will respond.

"The Holocaust was World War II," Abe explains. "That's it. Just a time in history that was really horrible."

"Okay, so what's this other *holocaust*?" Brad asks.

(Continued)

Certain there is no difference, Abe, who is fascinated by anything related to the military, says, "There isn't any difference."

"You mean the word came into being at this time in history? That it was created to define World War II?" wonders Brad.

Suddenly a little unsure, Abe shrugs. McKenzie begins to slump in her chair, rethinking her earlier comment.

"Okay, let's take a look at the words. Why do you think one is capitalized and the other isn't?"

"Well, the capitalized one means the time period in World War II, like Abe said," James says.

"True. So what's the other one mean?"

After no student offers a response, Brad says, "The word *holocaust* means a complete destruction of something caused by fire. Some definitions refer to it as a sacrifice by fire. Others add that it involves significant loss of life. So there are other types of holocausts beyond the one associated with World War II—say, a nuclear holocaust. But, yes, we do refer to this time period in history as the Holocaust. What's the relationship between Holocaust with a capital *H* and holocaust with a lowercase *h*? Sadly, World War II is not the only example of a holocaust in the world's history. Have any of you seen *Hotel Rwanda*, in which the main character hides refugees trying to escape persecution? That's another example of a holocaust. So, what do you think the relationship might be?"

"I heard that Hitler ordered people to be gassed and burned to kill them, which fits with what you said the word means," James says. "So maybe that's it."

"Or maybe it's because Hitler raged through the Jewish population, killing everyone he could find," Brittany suggests. "That fits with what you said about 'significant loss of life.'"

"I think it's because the Jewish population in Germany and surrounding countries was practically wiped out," Julie, a self-proclaimed poet, adds dully.

"These are all great thoughts," Brad says, "and I think you have the idea." After continuing through the remaining words, he says, "I think we have a good handle on what these words mean on the surface, but I think as we study them, you will learn that many describe really deep concepts—like we saw with holocaust. You will also notice that some of the words we're studying don't actually appear in the text, but understanding them will help us more thoroughly make sense of the text."

Brad distributes the Probable Passage organizer and explains that before they start reading *The Diary of Anne Frank*, the students will be reading an excerpt from a book by one of the people who helped to hide her and her family. He asks students to sort the words and to determine some questions they think such a passage will answer.

Figure 5.4 shows what Carrie's paper looks like.

Context	People	Problem
extraordinary times Auschwitz Bergen-Belsen Holocaust	Dutch Jews innocence Nazi	tyranny invansion betrayal innocence Nazi anti-Semitism holocaust
Causes & Effects	**Solutions**	**Questions I think the text will answer**
ordinary people extraordinary times gratitude invasion	ordinary people invasion	• How did ordinary people survive in extraordinary times? What did they do? • Why is gratitude an emotion during the Holocaust? • Who betrayed whom? Why? • In what way is an invasion a problem AND a solution?

Words to be studied:

Dutch	ordinary people	Auschwitz	holocaust
Jews	extraordinary times	Bergen-Belsen	gratitude
tyranny	innocence	anti-Semitism	invasion
betrayal	Nazi	Holocaust	

Figure 5.4   *Nonfiction Probable Passage—Anne Frank*

Notice that although many of the words do not actually appear in the text, Carrie is able to get a sense of the passage to be read and to ask some thoughtful questions that will set her schema for reading.

Differentiation: Step into a History Classroom

One of the most beneficial aspects to the Probable Passage strategy is that it is easily used and adapted across disciplines, allowing kids to use the same strategy in many contexts. Such cross-disciplinary use helps kids maximize reading strategies as they encounter various types of text.

Next door, students in Joanie's classroom are preparing to read the Declaration of Independence. She, too, has prepared a Probable Passage. The words on her board read: *entitle, denounce, government, dissolve, endeavored, political bands, relinquish, representation, protect, United States, honor, king, Great Britain, colonies, elected, tyranny, taxes,* and *trade.*

Because Joanie feels that her students will need more practice and guidance to gain conceptual understanding of these terms, she elects to do this activity as a whole class. Using an electronic whiteboard (a whiteboard hooked up to a computer), Joanie projects the words onto the screen next to an electronic version of the Probable Passage organizer. (Before getting an electronic whiteboard in her classroom, Joanie used an overhead projector for this activity, but the whiteboard allows her to print a copy of the group's work, allowing students to really focus on discussion rather than copying the information into their notes.)

When students get to *Great Britain* the discussion elevates. "*Great Britain* goes under people, Ms. Williams," Sydney says.

"No, it goes under problem," Desmond counters.

"No, it's a place. It goes under setting," Carol says.

"But the American Revolution didn't take place in Great Britain. The colonists left Great Britain because they felt oppressed. Great Britain is the problem," Desmond insists.

Joanie resolves this by allowing *Great Britain* to be included in multiple boxes, and the class decides to put it under problem and people.

When finished, the information on the whiteboard looks like Figure 5.5. While students' understandings of the words vary in complexity, the discussion prompts each of them to broaden their image of these words. In what ways can a country be a problem? Would citizens of that country see themselves that way? When does the country stand for all of the individuals associated with it? As the class learns more about the founding of our nation and continues to work with these words, Joanie will ask these questions, and others, to help deepen her students' conceptual understanding.

Conceptual Sorts

Sorting and re-sorting teaches kids that ideas are dynamic. For example, when I taught ninth-grade English, I was required to teach *Romeo and Juliet.* Wanting the students to understand that the main characters could

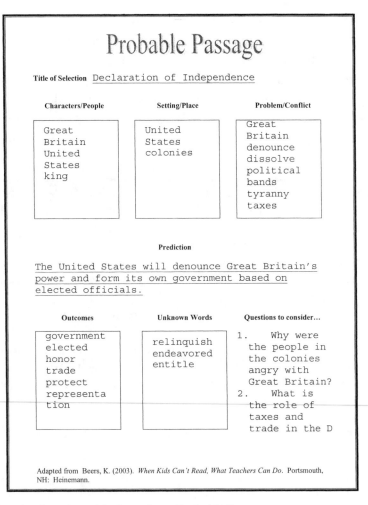

Probable Passage

Title of Selection Declaration of Independence

Characters/People	Setting/Place	Problem/Conflict
Great Britain United States king	United States colonies	Great Britain denounce dissolve political bands tyranny taxes

Prediction

The United States will denounce Great Britain's power and form its own government based on elected officials.

Outcomes	Unknown Words	Questions to consider…
government elected honor trade protect representa tion	relinquish endeavored entitle	1. Why were the people in the colonies angry with Great Britain? 2. What is the role of taxes and trade in the D

Adapted from Beers, K. (2003). *When Kids Can't Read, What Teachers Can Do.* Portsmouth, NH: Heinemann.

Figure 5.5   *Declaration of Independence Probable Passage*

be examined through many lenses, we sorted and re-sorted the cast list throughout our study of the play. At first we simply sorted the characters into the houses with which they were associated, necessitating the categories *Capulet, Montague,* and *Other.* This sort allowed students to become familiar with the characters' outward allegiances. As our study progressed, we re-sorted those same characters into different categories based on various elements of their personalities. One sort was based on the categories *Peacekeepers, Troublemakers,* and *Neither.* Another group of categories we used was *For the Marriage, Against the Marriage,* and *Neutral.* As we examined the characters through different lenses, we came to appreciate their complexity. It was through these re-sorts that students learned to view Friar Laurence, whom students often initially interpret as a kindly fellow (teenagers always root for Romeo and Juliet to "hook up" and the friar assists in that endeavor), as a troublemaker who plays a clear role in creating the story's tragedy. The characters became real, fleshed-

STEP INTO A MATHEMATICS CLASSROOM

John's algebra class is reviewing for the semester exam. They have learned how to solve equations with numerical representations, to read and solve inequalities, and to look at the relationships in mathematical procedures. Wanting to review some of the semester's terminology, John prepares a conceptual sort with the following words: *addition, subtraction, multiplication, division, expression, inequality, variable, integer, value, constant,* π, and *x.*

During class, John distributes a previously prepared envelope containing these words to each student. He asks the students to sort the words in a way that is logical to them and to write their sort categories and words on a sheet of paper. Zalie quickly sorts the words in the broadest categories she can think of. Pleased to be finished first, she begins to doodle on her notebook. Adding the category headings, her sort looks like this:

Operations	Equations	Other
addition	expression	inequality
subtraction	variable	
multiplication	integer	
division	value	
	constant	
	π	
	x	

As John circulates around the room, he notices Zalie's quick sort. He gives her a quick, smile, knowing that she may not be as done as she thinks she is, and moves on. After a couple of minutes, John tells the students to re-sort the words, saying they must find different categories.

Irritated but determined, Zalie begins to consider more thoughtfully the words before her. She starts to move them around, but gets stuck when the categories begin to mimic her initial thinking. John says, "Keep at it, Zalie. Are any of those processes related?" and walks to the other side of the room, leaving her to struggle through this activity, but knowing that she has the content knowledge and understanding to be successful. Finally, Zalie has these categories:

Related Operations	Related Operations	Numbers	Problems
addition	multiplication	integer	expression
subtraction	division	variable	inequality
		value	
		x	
		constant	
		π	

Although initially frustrated, Zalie completes the task, and in doing so, begins to think about new relationships among the vocabulary. As the new groupings emerged, Zalie began to understand the possible multiple relationships and became more fully aware of the inverse processes that she has internalized through years of working mathematical problems.

out, and dynamic. Conceptual sorts afford kids opportunities to deepen their understanding of the nuances, connotations, and multiple meanings of words.

Setup

The method of setting up and using this strategy will depend largely on the text or information at hand. When reading a novel, for example, working with characters' names and sorting them throughout the study will help bring to light the traits that make the characters dynamic or flat.

With nonfiction text, however, you may elect to use key vocabulary, prepared in the same way as you'd prepare for the Probable Passage activity. The key to selecting words for this strategy is to ensure that the words can be categorized and recategorized. You may also include key terms related to the discipline and have students sort and re-sort those.

Before beginning this activity, read the text at hand and select ten to twenty words to be sorted. Write or type the words on paper. If creating a text document, put the words in a table (the grid lines make these easy to cut evenly). Cut out the words (or have students do this). Make sure that each student or group of students will have a complete set of words. To keep word groups together, I use envelopes, which allows me to write group names on the outside. When I use sorts with multiple classes that may be at different points in a text or studying the same text at different times in the year, this maximizes material use while making the various sorts easy to identify.

Differentiation

You will need to choose whether to provide students with category headings. In the *Romeo and Juliet* example, I provided the categories based on which portion of the text we were discussing. Providing headings makes the conceptual sort significantly easier than if students must read the words and determine their own headings.

STEP INTO A PHYSICAL EDUCATION CLASSROOM

Mary's students are also reviewing for the semester exam. Although the majority of their work will be performance based, Mary will also be giving a pencil-and-paper semester exam. Wanting to go beyond the simple rules of sports they have played through the term, Mary uses a conceptual sort to help kids see relationships among the activities they've learned. Mary has posted the following words on the wall of the gym: *soccer, basketball, rock climbing, tennis, croquet, field hockey, tumbling, balance, base of support, badminton, flexibility, endurance,* and *volleyball*. In addition, she has made index cards with the words and put students in teams to work on the various sorts. Although the students will work together to create their groupings, she asks them to record their categories on their individual papers for reference when studying.

Kelly's initial sort looks like this:

Team Sports	Individual Sports	Conditioning
soccer	rock climbing	balance
basketball	tennis	base of support
tennis	croquet	flexibility
field hockey	tumbling	endurance
volleyball		

When asked to re-sort, Kelly's paper reads:

Sports with a Ball	Equipment to Hit with	Central Net	Other
soccer	tennis	tennis	rock climbing
basketball	croquet	badminton	tumbling
tennis	badminton	volleyball	balance
volleyball			base of support
croquet			flexibility
			endurance

In yet a third sort, Kelly comes up with this:

Flexibility	Balance	Endurance	Base of Support
rock climbing	tennis	soccer	croquet
tumbling	rock climbing	basketball	rock climbing
	tumbling	tennis	tumbling
		volleyball	
		badminton	
		rock climbing	

Not only does each sort challenge Kelly to think about the traits of these sports and fitness terms but it also provides insight for Mary, allowing her to uncover Kelly's understandings as well as her misconceptions.

Visual Front-Loading

Just like it sounds, "visual front-loading" of vocabulary involves providing learners with images, usually in the form of photographs or video, to call upon when learning new terms or reading difficult text. The Zeffirelli-directed *Romeo and Juliet*, for example, shows one artist's vision of the Capulet's monument. It is a building; it is not a series of graveyard plots. Seeing this helps students to understand burial traditions, and through this, they can see how the Friar's plan to reunite the young lovers is plausible. This strategy, especially when applied to text, provides kids with images that they can easily call to mind when encountering new words in the context of their reading. This allows them to use the cognitive energy they save (by not needing to puzzle through each word's meaning) to focus on the deeper meaning of the passage as a whole.

Setup

Visually front-loading text requires planning. Teachers must find those visual aids that will paint a clear picture in the learner's mind. Clearly the Internet and video streaming have made this easier, but it still takes time to find accurate representations. Although finding the photographs and video clips that will help students to keep images in their mind when reading can be time-consuming, the effort pays off when students delve into difficult text, excited to truly experience and analyze how authors craft meaning.

STEP INTO A CLASSROOM

Let's return to Shakespeare for a moment. When teaching *Romeo and Juliet*, I broke the unwritten code of *always* watching a film *after* reading the text. We watched, analyzed, and discussed each section of the play *before* reading. Why? Because early modern English throws kids for a loop.

Did I ruin the surprise ending? No. Even Shakespeare's Prologue tells the reader what will happen. The point of reading the play is to find out the how and the why. It's to get the real scoop. Beyond that, when students already have conceptual information in their minds, they can also experience the beauty of blank verse and Shakespeare's expertise as an enchanting storyteller.

But how can kids accomplish that if they spend all of their cognitive energy focusing on trying to understand enough of the language to make sense of the plot, rather than looking at how Shakespeare uses words and word play to convey deeper meaning?

For example, in this particular text, Romeo's tragic error is killing Tybalt. When reading the text, kids generally understand that, angry over Mercutio's death at Tybalt's hand, Romeo challenges Tybalt to a fight to the death. Those words are pretty clear. Kids often miss, however, the intentions of the fight between Mercutio and Tybalt. Mistakenly, they often assume that this is also a fight to the death. The words in the text provide clues, but visually front-loading this scene helps tremendously.

In the Zeffirelli version of the film, as Tybalt and Mercutio's conflict escalates, we see the characters from the two houses (dressed in full doublets and jackets) beginning to toss insults around. At the center of the fray, Tybalt and Mercutio draw swords. But wait—everyone is still smiling. Everyone is still fully dressed. The crowd forms a circle around them, each side cheering on their man. At one point, Tybalt cuts off a lock of Mercutio's hair with his sword. Daggers are still in their sheaths. This isn't a fight to the death; this is just boyish one-upmanship. Tybalt *accidentally* kills Mercutio, unable to gauge the depth of his thrust under the peacemaker Romeo's arm.

When Tybalt and Romeo fight, however, they strip down to their shirts, allowing for greater freedom of movement. Both swords and daggers are pulled, and the crowd joins in the fight, each trying to gain a point of advantage for their man. When Romeo loses his sword, he calls for another. His friends try to help him, and Tybalt's friends work to prevent this assistance. Clearly, this is meant to be a real sword fight with real consequences, right from the start. Imagine how this scene will be illuminated for students as they read if they already have clear images of each fight in their minds when they begin.

At another point in the text, Friar Laurence schemes to help Juliet feign death by putting her into a deep sleep, and to smuggle Romeo into the Capulet's tomb so that he is there when she awakes. For students with a contemporary American notion of burial, envisioning the type of vault Shakespeare had in mind as he wrote will be very difficult. How many students think Romeo has gone mad when he starts addressing Tybalt in the Capulet's tomb? He's not seeing a ghost; he's seeing Tybalt's decaying body. Showing this scene from a video, sharing pictures of these large family monuments, and discussing burial rites *before reading the scene* allows students to focus on what is actually happening when Romeo enters the tomb rather than trying to determine how such a feat is even possible.

What Are the Signs?

Yes, a little visualization frees up cognitive space for students to play with the language they encounter. But what happens when we want to visually front-load the words themselves? Sure, pictures and video are still available, but that can take a lot of precious time for a small list of words. Learning and teaching a little sign language is another strategy to visually front-load conceptual meaning and specific language.

American Sign Language bases itself in conceptual or root meanings of words. Although there are thousands of signs, the number doesn't begin to approach the number of words in the English language. Moreover, many of those signs are actually combinations of other signs. For example, I was preparing to sign a song for our Easter Sunday service and noticed that none of the American Sign Language dictionaries I consulted carried a specific sign for the word *throne*. When I asked a friend who works in the deaf community to help me with the interpretation of the word, she asked first about the context and situation.

"If you are teaching someone what a throne is, you would use a combination of many signs to describe a chair. They might include the sign for *fancy* combined with the sign for *chair* (actually the same sign for *sit*). If you will be referring to the throne of royalty, you should combine the signs for *king* and *chair*."

Thinking about the signs used actually deepens our understanding of the word throne: It *is* a *fancy chair* or a place where the *king sits*. Paying attention to this simple combination of representative signs helps kids think about a word's original intent.

Learning some simple signs also allows students to interact physically with language (in much more productive ways than acting out random words!) while creating visual representations of words.

Using the previous example, the sign for *king* is the *k* sign moving from the left shoulder to the right hip, forming a sort of sash. The sign for *queen* is the same except using a *q* sign. In this way, students understand not only that royalty may be denoted by emblems but also that *king* and *queen* are related.

In the same way, American Sign Language uses what's known as a *person marker*, meaning there is one sign that transforms many other signs to refer to an individual as opposed to an action. The sign for *save*, for example, is made starting with both hands signing *s* and "bound" in a crossed position over the chest. The arms are then opened ("unbound") and moved to the shoulders. To sign *savior*, we simply add the person marker by sliding open palms downward from the chest to the waist. What do kids gain from learning these two signs? First, they see that to save something means to free it, to "unbind" it in some way. Second, a *savior* is a person who frees something.

Setup

Don't think that you need to be fluent in sign language to make this strategy work in your classroom. As seen in the example, I'm not fluent and ask trusted resources for assistance when I am uncertain of signs.

First, it's likely that someone in your school—a teacher or a student—knows sign language. If so, work with that individual to learn some basic signs. The idea here isn't the complexity of the words but that the signs will help students to see words in a new way. Second, get an American Sign Language dictionary and look up signs for some of the common words in English. Learn signs like *us*, *we*, *I*, and *you*, and think about how their visualization will help students to better visualize meanings of words.

When preparing lessons and considering the key vocabulary my students must master in order to be successful, I often consult a sign language dictionary to see if the visual representation of a word will help students to learn the word. Because I use this tool throughout the year, but without the intent of actually teaching sign language, I weave the strategy into lessons when the visual representation may be the difference between truly understanding a word and just memorizing a definition.

Sometimes I use this strategy to create a sense of play around words, like with the word *throne*. In these situations, I may teach several signs, like *king*, *sit*, and *fancy*, and then challenge students to interpret *throne*.

Julie, a high school sophomore, volunteers at an after-school program in her school district working with primary students on language acquisition. On this fall Tuesday, Julie is teaching a group of five- and six-year-olds how to sign pronouns.

"Boys and girls, I have noticed that these funny little words called pronouns can be really confusing, so today I want to play a little game to help us remember them because they are important in our language for referring to people we know. But first, let's review our sign language alphabet because we will be using these letters a lot for our game."

"Hands up. A-b-c . . ." Julie and her students recite the alphabet while making the appropriate letter signs.

"Wonderful! The signs we are going to learn today are words we use in place of someone's name. For example, instead of saying 'Julie and the class went to the store,' I can say, 'We went to the store.' See how I switched *we* for *Julie and the class*? Today we are going to learn that some of these words include whoever is speaking and some of them do not. The signs help us see which is which. As we go over these words, I want you to think about why these signs might look the ways they do."

"First, let's learn the sign for *us*. To make this sign, you will use your *u*." Instantly, seven sets of little fingers fly into the air in the *u* sign.

"Good. We are going to start with our *u* at our right shoulders. Then we are going to make a half circle to bring that *u* to our left shoulders. Like this." Julie demonstrates for the children and then they practice making the sign.

"Okay. Now let's make another sign that includes the person who's talking. This is the sign for *we*. To make this sign, let's start with our *w* in the same place— by the right shoulder. Now let's make the same motion as we did for *us*."

As the children practice making the two signs, Julie asks, "Do you notice anything special about these signs?"

"They both make sort of a circle," Anthony exclaims, practically popping off the floor where the children are seated in a circle.

"Yeah, kind of like halfway around our circle," Rosemary agrees.

"Great. So if I were to start with where I am sitting and make a circle around where we are sitting until I get back to me, would I include all of us in it?"

"Yes!"

"So let's think about our signs: They make a circle that includes the person making the sign. So *us* and *we* include everyone in the group that is being talked about."

The lesson moves on to signs for *you*, *them*, *her*, and so on. All of these signs move away from the body, indicating that the speaker is not included. In short,

Julie helps the children to create word pictures that help them to visualize word meanings.

Teaching students to visualize and conceptualize words requires that teachers can also visualize and conceptualize words. In this case, Julie helps students to categorize the words they are learning by calling attention to words that include the speaker and words that exclude the speaker.

In Summary

When it comes to conceptual meaning makers, kids often need help not only to learn the words and their definitions but to truly understand *why* and *how* the words are significant to the text at hand. By bringing those words to students' attention *before* reading and continuing to work with them as appropriate throughout the course of study, students will be better able to internalize new vocabulary, greatly enhancing their understanding of the topic.

Extending Concepts During and After Reading

While front-loading vocabulary is important when encouraging students to make meaning of text as they read, it's just as vital that we keep those words in front of students until they are mastered. Too often the words we initially highlighted are closed in with the final pages of the book. Helping kids retain that rich, new vocabulary as well as helping them transfer those words into their writing can be a real challenge.

If we highlight the conceptual meaning makers of a text—instead of just the most difficult words—they will continue to be of use throughout a student's time in school, as they come up again and again in texts. Still, new words might not be encountered with sufficient frequency to keep those words active in kids' minds as they read them. For this reason, students benefit from having multiple opportunities to use those conceptual meaning makers in their writing.

The following activities are designed to provide support as students learn and use new vocabulary.

Formula Poems

Although formula poems are traditionally used to emphasize and provide practice with parts of speech, teachers can easily adapt them to reinforce concepts related to the topic they are currently studying as well as the conceptual vocabulary associated with that topic.

Setup

The teacher writes the formula, or template, for the poem on the board. Because the point of the activity is to reinforce key vocabulary, the formulas should remain straightforward. I typically use the following three formulas: *Noun-Verb-Adverb*, *Adjective-Noun-Verb*, and *Adjective-Noun-Verb-Adverb*. Students write four lines that each follow the formula you have chosen and then add an ending line using a prepositional phrase. If students are still learning parts of speech, reviewing nouns, verbs, adjectives, adverbs, and prepositional phrases will be necessary.

For example, a simple *Noun-Verb-Adverb* poem might read:

> Clouds swirl menacingly
> Wind whips purposefully
> Objects fly randomly
> Tornado roars sinisterly
>   through the Kansas field.

STEP INTO A CLASSROOM

Joe's sixth-grade health students have been learning about nutrition labels and how different nutrients behave in the body. In order to review, Joe breaks the class into groups and assigns each group a category (fats, cholesterol, carbohydrates, protein, and vitamins/minerals). Each group will present a project to explain the benefits and drawbacks of their category. One portion of that project will be a formula poem.

Jerome, Liza, Toni, Paul, and Kari have the category *fat*. As they organize their information, Kari grumbles that it isn't fair that their group is in charge of something so gross.

"But fat isn't necessarily gross," Paul counters. "You need some fat, and there are good fats that help the body."

"Right," Jerome adds. "Fats help you to feel full."

"And nuts and fish have good fats," Liza adds.

(Continued)

"But there's also all that fat hanging off of meat. And lard. Ewwww!" Kari squeals. "I don't think I can ever eat meat again after seeing some of those pictures in our book."

"Let's start by making a list of words we should include," the ever-organized Liza suggests.

The students brainstorm the following list of words related to their topic: *saturated, monounsaturated, polyunsaturated, lard, fatty acid, cholesterol, omega 3, omega 6, shortening, olive oil, potato chips, butter, fish, heart disease, arteries.*

Using the words from their list and other words from their notes, the students write this poem to present to the class:

> Food fried deeply
> Arteries clog slowly
> Cholesterol accumulates dangerously
> Heart pumps rapidly
>   from too much saturated fat.

Although the poem is simple, the students demonstrate an understanding of the connection between food and overall health.

Working with conceptual meaning makers often means that students must understand both multiple contexts and connotative meanings for the learned vocabulary. The following strategies help students to play with words in figurative ways to better understand their denotative meanings.

Go Figure!

When I first moved to Georgia, the wealth of unfamiliar figurative language—especially regional idioms like *put on the dog* (to make a show of wealth)—threw me for a loop (oops, there's another one!). In many ways, it was like a different language. The figurative rather than literal uses of words were sometimes new to me, and I often had to think conceptually about the words to understand the phrases. In the example of *put on the dog*, there are two possible origins that help to make sense of the phrase. The first claims that the wealthy once owned shoes made of dog skin (yuck!) and that when invited to a fancy party, one would wear one's best shoes. The other claimed origin (which is much more palatable in my mind) comes from the rise of popularity in lap dogs, which are typically viewed as pristine and pampered and intended to be shown off. Either potential origin helps to put a picture in one's mind, and when I imagine Fido with a diamond collar, hair bows, and a crystal dish filled with food, I can visualize the ostentatious display of wealth and, thus, have a better understanding of the phrase.

So much of understanding and being able to manipulate the English language depends on being able to both unpack the meaning of and create one's own figurative associations. It is important that we provide kids with plenty of opportunities to play with figurative language and to practice using it effectively in their own writing. This activity helps expose students to many examples of figurative language, allowing them to think through the expressions' meanings as well as providing them with material to work into their own writing.

Setup

To begin, brainstorm with your students a list of idioms, discussing their figurative meanings as well as their literal interpretations. I always start by sharing examples of idioms that are easy to visualize when taken literally, like *hit the road*. I might tell students of a time when my daughter, in her terrible twos, was angry that I made her stay in her car seat while we were driving home. As soon as she was unbuckled, she performed the classic spread eagle on the driveway, beating her fists and kicking her little feet. Literally, she *hit the road*. When we use the term in everyday speech, we certainly don't want anyone to endanger his life actually beating the pavement in the middle of the street. When provided with clear examples of denotation (literal meaning) and connotation (figurative meaning), students more easily understand the difference between the two.

After students have generated a good list of idioms—ones they can visualize easily and relate to (when teaching multiple sections of a course, I keep a running list across classes)—distribute blank paper, and ask them to draw both the literal and figurative meanings of an idiom of their choice.

Figure 6.1 *Idiom Picture—Apple Pie*

Students may have trouble creating images for both the literal and figurative meanings, so to get them started I share an example that I created (see Figure 6.1).

Generally seeing even one example and reviewing a class-generated list of idioms will help students understand the difference between literal and figurative meanings. Then students can create their own pictures for various idioms. In this example (Figure 6.2), Alex has worked with the phrase *to be in hot water*.

Later, post these pictures around the room, and use them as examples when you challenge students to use idioms to make their writing more image-filled and lively for the reader.

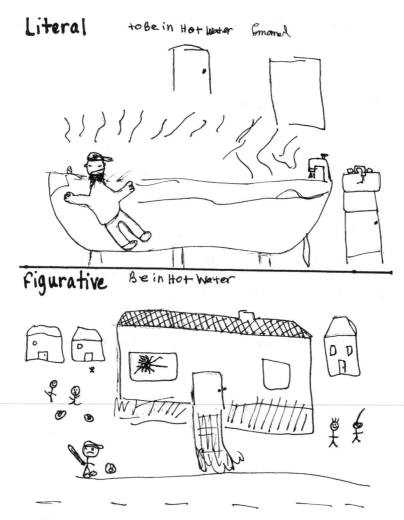

Figure 6.2   *Idiom Picture—To Be in Hot Water*

The same activity can be used for similes, metaphors, and personification. In particular, personification lends itself to drawing the figurative meaning because the images can be very funny. Most people have seen at least one cartoon with *time flying*, generally represented with a clock thrown from a window.

Susan's students' idiom pictures are displayed around her classroom above the board, providing easy viewing access during writer's workshop. Today, students are revising a piece of writing to include figurative language. Susan challenges the kids to include at least two idioms or other types of figurative language (metaphor, simile, or personification) to enrich their writing.

McKenzie's account of a rainstorm when she was in Hawaii visiting the Seven Sacred Pools is interesting because the place itself is dramatic, but overall her writing is rather ordinary. During a writer's conference, Susan asks McKenzie, "What are some of the places in your narrative that you could use figurative language to help make the description more lively?"

"I don't know. I can see it so clearly in my head, but my writing group said that the images are a little difficult to see."

"Okay. Did your group mention anything specific, or do you have a section you would like to discuss with me?"

"I think it sounds like it was just an average rainy day, but it wasn't. It was pouring rain," McKenzie explained, "which is what I wrote."

"Pouring how? There are so many kinds of rain—was this like a sudden, quick shower that is over in a few minutes or was it raining so hard that you couldn't see through it?"

"So hard we couldn't see through it. So I guess you could say it was raining cats and dogs, but I don't like that one because everyone says it, and it doesn't seem to fit the setting."

"Okay. Is there another idiom we have displayed that might work better?"

McKenzie scans the room and then says, "We were drenched to the bone." A grin spreads across her face as she recalls her soaking clothes, squeaky shoes, and matted hair. It's perfect.

Kids won't always find the best idiom on the wall, and idioms alone don't bring writing to life. As teachers, we should help students to use the examples as idea generators rather than the answers themselves. The answers live in each writer, and as students recall new and exciting phrases, they should add them, if only in a list format.

Differentiation

Figurative associations can present significant problems for English Language Learners. Although most languages use idioms of their own, the phrases often vary from American phrases. Even in English, the British,

Scottish, Irish, or Australian sayings vary from their American counterparts. For example, the Scots say, "It's folly to live poor to dee rich," while Americans would say, "You can't take it with you!" Limiting this activity to common American idioms, which can be difficult with regional variations, will help students master those idioms they are likely to encounter when speaking with their peers.

Another way to provide more structure for those students who need it is to ask them to write a dialogue between two students—a situation ripe for use of idioms. Even having students write a quick phone conversation about going out with friends will include idioms like *What's up?* and *Catch you later!* Not only will this make the writing portion of the assignment simpler, it will allow students to test out context for various idioms in a fun format and with other students who are learning idioms, thus providing a safe environment.

Another way to play with figurative language is to twist the truth using connotative associations with words.

Load It Up

Last year I took my eight-year-old to see the new *Scooby Doo* movie. From watching the original cartoons, she already loved the characters and knew that the story would revolve around some thrilling mystery to be solved. The story in this movie is set on a resort island, where the main characters quickly notice that something about their vacation destination isn't quite right. The other guests seem a little odd, and strange things keep happening. Scooby and company begin to put together the clues—the connotations, if you will—and form a plan for understanding the unsettling aspects of this vacation destination: dazed, zombie-like tourists and a spooky legend.

Just as we put together clues to solve a mystery in a movie, when students are reading, they must be cognizant of loaded language and the clues it can provide to the author's purpose. To teach this, I often have students analyze the language usage in two articles—one from a conservative publication like *Newsweek* and one from a more liberal publication like *Time*—on the same topic. Through such activities, students began to see that everything is a matter of perspective.

Presidential elections always provide excellent examples of loaded language and author bias/perspective. Before the primaries, candidates are technically running against people in their own party, but that's not the whole story. Ultimately, one of those candidates will go on to run against someone in another party, so opposing parties often use loaded language to describe each other's candidates. The underlying belief is that if group A can make the lead candidate in group B look weak, the final race will be less challenging.

While my students grew stronger with recognizing loaded language in the articles we studied, they often still struggled to identify their own use of loaded language as they wrote. Even when writing persuasive essays, kids presented their own biases as fact rather than recognizing that they could use particular words to present an argument based on opinion. To help kids both to recognize the loaded language they were already using and to learn to use language effectively, I designed writing assignments to encourage strong vocabulary usage through the art of persuasion.

In one assignment, I found pictures of run-down mansions (cobwebs, loose boards, weeds, and all) and asked students to assume these ruins were bed and breakfast inns. We brainstormed other details to add as well—that the mansions were haunted, had no air-conditioning, contained shabby curtains, and the like. As marketing agents for the owners of the mansions with the goal of maximizing reservations, they were to create a series of brochures to distribute to prospective guests. One student opened her brochure with "A step back in time . . ." while another student started, "Authentic 1800s Home with original detailing . . ." Students enjoyed the creative aspects of the writing—trying to find clever ways to create positive images in the readers' minds without actually lying about the condition of the homes.

Setup

This type of writing can be set up in a variety of ways. Some teachers choose to give students a bulleted list of things they "observed" when "visiting"

Ms. Evans' physics students are designing different attractions at the Abominable Amusement Park. Each one is to create and market an attraction based on unsound engineering decisions, thus making it unrealistic and unsafe. Collectively, their attractions will form the class' amusement park. Their descriptive papers about their attractions must include specific physics terminology.

When completed, Ms. Evans will ask students to trade papers, to analyze the attractions, and to use what they know about the principles of physics to redesign each ride to make it safe.

A roller coaster fanatic, Billy is designing a triple-loop coaster that combines aspects of a traditional coaster with a water coaster (or log ride). He's excited about the possibility of designing a ride that sends people both upside down *and* through water. The easiest way to make the ride unsound is to design loops that follow lower slopes on the ride, so that not enough centrifugal force will be created to carry the coaster all the way through, thus making it fall off the track and plummet to the ground. He adds this feature but also wants to include a less obvious engineering error. He includes a track that runs in a sideways arc through the water and into an elliptical loop. This arc comes immediately after the main drop into the water and doesn't allow enough time for the coaster to level out before turning; thus, according to his calculations, the coaster will flip off the track. This portion of Billy's paper reads:

> After dropping 262 feet on an angled slope through both a spray of water over the coaster and the pool of water at the bottom of the low exiting slope, a secondary thrill awaits riders. An immediate and tight arc will launch the coaster into an elliptical lo\op, leaning riders upside-down over the pool of water, before leveling out and curving back around the pool. Even the most veteran thrill seekers will scream in delight as the coaster finally pulls into the docking station.

Such writing activities provide opportunities for students to apply terminology in real-life scenarios, thus requiring them to think like experts in the field think and to use the correct language to describe their projects. This also provides an opportunity for students to synthesize their content knowledge as they apply information to novel contexts.

Aside from applying vocabulary, it is important that students have opportunities to play with academic language for the sheer joy of words. Because our academic language in English derives largely from Latin and Greek, this next activity will encourage play with some basic etymology as well as with the words themselves.

some place, real or fictional, and have kids create a piece of writing (letters and brochures work well) to describe that place. This method of providing statements, like *the floor boards creak*, helps students to have examples of figurative language. Giving pictures to students, on the other hand, provides the visual without language examples. I find that the picture method works well to assist students who have difficulty forming and holding onto a consistent mental image.

Teachers can also require that specific terminology be included in the writing sample. For example, a history teacher might require that the writing be set in a specific time period or include correct geographical terms.

Earlier this year I visited Charleston, South Carolina, and had the "opportunity" to take a ghost tour. (I was basically dragged into it.) One of the things that struck me—aside from the flash bulbs from people trying to catch a ghost on camera—was that the tour guide used modern phrases and terminology to describe the old (1800s) city jail, commenting that the building didn't have air-conditioning. But in the 1800s, building construction and fans would have also aided in keeping a building cool, even in the Charleston summer heat.

Who's Your Daddy?

I love teaching Ancient Greek literature. Sophocles, Homer, Euripides—all favorites. Why? I'm fascinated with the Greeks not only because of their various contributions to society—government, literature, architecture, philosophy—but also because their ideas have stood the test of time. Our modern English linguistic and literary traditions reach back to the Greeks, something that has always piqued my interest.

When willing to investigate, one finds that many of the words we get from Greek (and Latin and French) originally had different meanings from those we are familiar with in contemporary usage. Translation matters: The same text may be interpreted in various ways, depending on the translator's cultural context, vocabulary knowledge, and choices they make. I first became aware of this in church when reading various translations of the

Bible. When considering that there are often multiple ways to translate words, as well as taking into account the context out of which translators are working, it's easy to see how translations of ancient texts (and contemporary texts as well) can differ, sometimes dramatically.

Recently I was visiting high school classrooms around our school system to gather student input about various textbooks we were considering adopting for our language arts curriculum. Having discussions with the kids who would use the books for learning provided considerable insight not only to students' opinions of the books but also to what they understood (and misunderstood) about the discipline of language arts.

One young lady approached me and declared, "This is the only book I like, and if I were you, this is the only book I'd buy."

"Why is that?" I prompted, curious about the reasoning behind her emphatic statement.

"Look here," she said, opening to a page with a poem by Sappho. "See, this one has *two* translations of this poem. All of the others have only one, and that's just stupid."

"Tell me what you mean," I said, becoming more and more impressed with this precocious sophomore.

"Well, this translation is by a man, and this one is by a woman. And they were both translated in the modern age."

"Okay. So?"

"Well, Sappho was a lesbian writing in Ancient Greece. So that's where she's coming from. And to understand the poem, we have to understand her cultural context. But we also need to look at where the translators are coming from, because they layer on their ideas and beliefs when they are choosing words. They see different things in the poem depending on who they are. So *this* translation is different from *this* one," she said, pointing to the text. "And because we don't speak Greek, it's important to look at lots of translations to get a better understanding of what the poem is saying."

"I see. And this is the only book that has multiple translations."

"Yep. I checked. For all of the translated material, this is the only one with multiple translations."

"And that's why we should buy this series?" I questioned.

It is September, and Kathryn is introducing the idea of word/etymology mapping to her language arts freshmen. Because they will read a number of ancient works throughout the year, she wants to introduce early the idea that words have histories and that mapping them helps us to better understand their meanings.

After introducing the genealogical approach to word mapping, Kathryn begins with an example.

"So, *love* is a word that we use in lots of different contexts to mean lots of different things, but did you know that the ancient Greeks actually used several different words to describe different types or elements of love?" Pausing to allow for the snickers the mention of love causes among fourteen-year-olds, Kathryn puts a basic word map on the overhead projector.

"Let's put *love* here in the top space. We won't always start this way, with the derived word. In fact, many times we will map words the other way, starting with a few synonyms (words that mean the same thing) and working our way back to the original word in Greek or Latin." She writes *love* at the top of the map and draws several lines spreading out under it. "So tell me some ways that you can love people."

Again pausing for snickers, one young gentleman, Skip, finally offers, "Well, like my mom. That's different from a girlfriend."

"Great! That's two different types of love. The girlfriend is a passionate love. The Greeks had a special word for that type of love—*eros.* Let's put that here." Kathryn writes *eros* under one of the lines. "But love between a parent and child is different. The Greeks had another word for that type of love—*storge.*" Kathryn again writes on the transparency.

"I love chocolate!" Phoebe offers.

"Okay. The Greeks liked good food, too. They referred to that as a general affection for something pleasing—*agape.*"

"Do any of you love your friends?" Kathryn continues.

"That's a girl thing," Jeremy chides.

"No, it's not. If you didn't have your baseball teammates, you'd be a lost puppy," Caroline says, rolling her eyes.

"Well, that kind of love, friendship love, is called *philia.*"

After writing the different Greek words on the overhead, Kathryn has the class help her add basic definitions. She continues, "So when we are reading, if the translation says *love,* why should we consider which of these terms the Greeks might have really used?"

> "I guess the different words would help us understand the relationships between characters, and that would help us better understand why they do things," Phoebe says.
>
> "I agree, Phoebe," says Kathryn. "Translators make choices. Sometimes they have many words to choose from and other times they have only one. Looking at the possibilities will help us to better understand what we read."

"That, and it's the only one with anything by David Mamet, and I think he's brilliant."

This conversation uncovers an amazing thought process. This student understands that words have multiple interpretations, and that various interpretations of words may lead a translator to choose words in the new language that may or may not fully represent what the author intended. They may be related, much like relatives on a genealogical chart, but they aren't exactly the same. Tracing the genealogical path—or origin to contemporary use—of words, or presenting multiple translations of the same text, helps students to understand the evolution of language and how it impacts conceptual understanding of text.

Setup

Make or find a genealogical chart to copy. (These are widely available online.) I prefer simple charts that allow me to focus on teaching the relationships on the chart rather than the more stylized ones that are made to look like actual trees (too crowded) and make assumptions about exact relationships (because the spaces for names and the connecting lines are preset). Use this chart to teach kids about how various relationships are represented—parent/child, spousal, sibling. When they are comfortable with this material, ask them each to make a basic genealogical chart representing their family, just to get a clear sense of how the charts work.

Next, introduce the chart's structure as a way to map the relationships between words as opposed to families. In some cases, English has multiple words to describe the same idea (*house* became *residence*, *theater*, *home*, and so

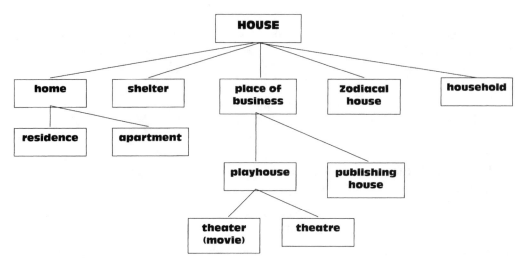

Figure 6.3   *Genealogical Chart of Words*

on) because those words were gathered from several different languages of origin, or because the original words split into several variations over time. Such words might be charted as in Figure 6.3.

Likewise, sometimes we find one word (*love* instead of *agape, philia,* and so on) that has multiple meanings. Often these words were initially described by several words in their languages of origin and were reduced to a single word in English as time passed. Charting words and word meanings helps kids to develop a conceptual picture of language. In this case, the chart will be inverted.

In Summary

Keeping conceptual meaning makers in front of kids so that they begin to internalize them requires extending key vocabulary knowledge beyond the text at hand. When kids have opportunities to continue to play with language as they do in these activities, they are more likely to master conceptual understanding of words and be able to relate that conceptual understanding to other existing contexts as well as in new contexts of their own creation.

SECTION THREE

Academic Vocabulary

Understanding: Readers and writers use context to determine a word's specific meaning.

Upon hearing the military march stream from the television, Ben looks up, curious as to the news story. This song always announces the President of the United States, he knows, although the title confuses him somewhat—"Hail to the Chief."

A Kansas native, Ben knows all about hail. When the ominous skies turn still and purple, Ben knows to head to the basement of their house. Such skies warn of tornadoes, which are generally preceded by heavy rain and hail, which plummets from the sky and ices the ground.

Why would anyone want hail to fall on the President? Or did people want to throw hail—or something like hail—at the President? And if that were the case, wouldn't the President have enough power to change the song that's played when he enters a room?

Confused, he calls, "Mom, why do they play that song 'Hail to the Chief'?"

"What do you mean, honey? It shows respect for the office of the President."

"Then why do people want hail to fall on him?"

Chuckling to herself, Ben's mom replies, "Hail has more than one meaning. It can mean the ice pellets that fall during a storm, which is what you are thinking about. But it can also mean to greet someone with enthusiasm, which is the case in the song."

"Oh, so when the President walks in, the people are saying hello!"

Why and How to Teach Academic Vocabulary

7

A few years ago, the importance of teaching academic vocabulary moved to the forefront of conversation about vocabulary instruction. Lists of academic words hit the Internet and teachers began to plan instruction around key words. Unfortunately, not everyone imagined the same word lists when using the term "academic vocabulary." Some believed that if we taught only those words that carry meaning across disciplines, kids could be successful on the standardized assessments required under No Child Left Behind. Indeed, those cross-disciplinary lists included many crucial words. *Analyze, compare, contrast, determine, synthesize,* and *conclude* all popped onto chalkboards and into student planners.

Simultaneously, other experts developed lists of terms that can mean very different things when related to different disciplines, and argued that students must know how to use these terms flexibly if they are to understand the discipline at hand. If, for example, a student doesn't recognize that the word *expression* in mathematics means one thing and in drama another, he will be unable to truly comprehend both disciplines. Marzano and Pickering (2005) contend that without understanding specific academic vocabulary, students will be unable to master the current year's content. They propose that teachers spend considerable time building students' background knowledge—that is, teaching missed vocabulary—so that kids will be successful.

Moreover, Marzano stresses that learning new academic terms—and words in general—should be connected to prior learning and word knowledge. How will students learn *simile* and *metaphor* without knowing the word *compare*? How will students distinguish between a tornado and a hurricane as they read if they have never experienced either?

When I was teaching in Kansas, most of my high school students had never been outside their home state. In fact, those who were new to our school in Wichita often commented on how overwhelming that huge city was to them, having moved from smaller towns and farm communities around the state. As a girl who had lived in Chicago, Denver, and Atlanta, I often found our varying perspectives frustrating as I attempted to help my students engage with the texts we were studying. Skyscrapers, oceans, beaches, enormous interstates, and air travel had been a part of my actual experience; they were not just things I'd seen in photographs, movies, television, or on the news, as they were to many of my students. So when working with new vocabulary, I needed to find ways to connect to my students' realities instead of just working with my own.

When students spend the majority of their school years within a single school system, aligned and spiraled curriculum can allow teachers to build on students' prior knowledge through curricular experiences. If, for example, I know that all students study the Holocaust in the seventh grade, I can draw on that knowledge when I teach *The Diary of Anne Frank* in eighth grade.

We live in an age of transience. Aside from making some sweeping generalizations based on age, we cannot assume that all students come to school with similar background knowledge and academic vocabulary. A middle school student who moves from Virginia to Texas during middle school will have been taught a great deal of information about Virginia history and very little about Texas history. In addition, that student will understand weather patterns and geography from the perspective of living in the Mid-Atlantic region of the nation, not from living in the Southwest. As teachers, we need to listen to our students to determine their background knowledge and understanding of academic language and build from that point.

We have a big task set for us! Logically, kids must know those words that carry meaning across disciplines. They must *also* know discipline-specific language and be able to use context to determine which meaning is appropriate. And they must be able to access an ever-growing bank of academic words as the content of their classes becomes more sophisticated. That's a lot of words!

Academic vocabulary lists are really extensions of the Fry lists (these lists of sight words and common academic words are based on the most frequent words in text). Unfortunately, many teachers believe that they alone are responsible for teaching their students every single word on every single list. Not true! Yes, we teachers should ensure that students know the vocabulary necessary to handle our course work, but that doesn't necessarily mean that we need to teach each word separately.

Our students aren't blank slates. They come to us already understanding and able to manipulate a wealth of words. The work we do on teaching vocabulary concepts can extend the knowledge that they already have. As I visit high school language arts classrooms, I notice that a lot of teachers still have kids define *noun*. They contend that the kids still don't know this information, and yet on our state standards, kids are tested on nouns in third grade. Sometimes I think kids are masters at pulling the wool over our eyes, claiming they have no knowledge just so they can repeat information they have already learned, ensuing an easy course. Other times, I see that kids may be able to recite that a noun is a person, place, thing, or idea, but they have little concept of how nouns function in sentences. Instead of beginning with the definition of nouns, we should add to that basic definition to the deeper understanding of how words work in sentences. This approach not only reinforces learned terminology but also makes that vocabulary more interesting to students.

It's often tempting to re-teach words kids learned years before (under the notion of review), but instead we should focus on teaching our students the terms that are necessary to understand the new information they are presented with. Whatever discipline we may teach, we have an obligation to teach contextual meanings—and to teach them before kids encounter the words in their daily work. With our colleagues, we need to form a pact to work together to teach the academic vocabulary that carries meaning across disciplines. Again, curriculum should guide decisions about which words to emphasize when.

When we use sophisticated terminology in our teaching, our students *will* rise to the occasion. Recently, I heard Kim Oliver, a National Board Certified Teacher and the 2006 Teacher of the Year, speak. She told a story about her kindergartners studying animals that live on land and animals that live in water. They were *comparing* and *contrasting* them, and she used that language in the classroom. Although most five-year-olds would use the simpler terms *same* and *different* if left to their own devices, this master teacher began building the academic language the children will encounter throughout their years in school.

Ultimately, we divide academic vocabulary into two categories: cross-disciplinary words and discipline-specific words. The following sections will introduce strategies for teaching both.

Cross-Disciplinary Words

Much of academic vocabulary is cross-disciplinary. These words often attempt to distinguish a level of analysis or understanding related to learning a discipline or concept. For example, are *analyze* and *evaluate* the same? Is one required for the other to occur? How are these terms related? Does one require more depth? If so, how? These are the questions students should ask when they encounter cross-disciplinary academic words. The following strategies help students to take ownership of these words and to use that understanding to grapple with the content at hand.

Levels of Meaning

All words are not created equal. If they were, we wouldn't have so many of them! We select words because of their connotative associations and denotative meanings, to express a specific idea or thought. As I write, I am surrounded by walls painted in *bright* blue, orange, and pink. I call it "the parrot room," and it serves as my office at home. I selected these colors and painted them on the wall in bold stripes offset by squiggly lines on the "seams." The inevitable question is *why?* The answer: I decided that if I am going to write a dissertation, I am going to do it in a room that is fun! When people visit our house, I am amused at their responses upon seeing my office for the first time. This room has been described as *fun, colorful, adorable, bright, outrageous,* and *whimsical.* Each of these words implies a different level of intensity. If I were to map them according to their nuances, beginning with the word with the most neutral meaning and progressing on in intensity, I might arrange them like this: *fun* (the most neutral), *adorable* (which can have a youthful and condescending connotation depending on its context but in this situation remains relatively neutral), *colorful, bright, whimsical* (which includes the connotation of color and fun), and *outrageous* (the most intense whether used in a positive or negative way).

When kids map words according to their levels of meaning as I've just done with the words describing my office, they get a better picture of the level of analysis or understanding the word implies. This strategy gives students greater access to the language of assessment questions, rubrics, and writing prompts.

Setup

Write an academic word on the chalkboard. Ask students to brainstorm words they associate with the selected word and list those to the side. As a class, determine if all of the brainstormed words truly relate to the given word and in what way. Students might say, for example, that to determine *significance* one must first *analyze* and *evaluate* something.

Have students work in groups to level the words, putting the most neutral word first (at the top for a vertical list or left for a horizontal list) and the most powerful word last (either bottom or right). As students work, they should discuss the connotations or definitions that prompt their decisions.

It is the first week of school, and Jim's ninth-grade students are working with some academic vocabulary words they will encounter throughout the year. From previous experience, Jim has learned that when he reviews and teaches early in the year some of the key terms his school system expects all freshmen to know, students will perform better throughout the year. As students enter the classroom on this hot August Thursday, they see the word *plausible* written on the board.

Jim begins the lesson saying, "Today we are going to work with some academic words that you already know. But instead of defining them, as many of you are accustomed to doing, we are going to think about relationships among these words. You see the word *plausible* written on the board. Let's brainstorm a list of words that we might associate with (or think about when we hear) the word *plausible*."

Students begin to call out words: *possible, likely, reasonable, actual, realistic, fair, valuable, probable, credible, believable, arguable.*

"That's a great list," Jim praises. "Do all of these words mean exactly the same thing?"

"No," Carrie answers.

"Why not?" Jim asks, seeking more information.

Carrie sighs, wishing he would ask another student. "If they all meant the same thing, we wouldn't have all those words."

"True. Can anyone select two of the words and tell me the difference between them?"

Brian, a willowy boy wearing cowboy boots says, "*Possible* and *likely* aren't the same. *Possible* means that something could happen, but it may not be likely to happen."

"Can you give me an example?"

"Sure," Brian continues. "It's possible that my parents will let me go to the movies Thursday night, but it isn't likely because it's a school night."

"Good. Can someone else distinguish between another pair?"

Ted, the sci-fi addict, says, "*Plausible* and *realistic* aren't exactly the same. I'm reading *Ender's Game*, and the main character, Ender, is a little kid who commands troops to fight aliens. It's plausible because I don't know what the future will be like and I guess it could happen, but it's not really realistic because it isn't real right now."

"Okay. So we have a sense that not all of these words mean exactly the same thing. Do we think all of them are related to the word *plausible*?" Jim asks.

"I guess if we looked in a thesaurus, we could find out if all of them are synonyms. That would tell us," Jessica replies.

"Yes, but I want you to make that determination on your own. What do you think, Jessica, are all of these related?"

"I guess so."

"Anyone disagree?" Being that it is the first week of school and Jim knows that his freshmen aren't likely to take many risks yet, he waits a bit but doesn't get a response. "Okay, well, let's try this: In your groups, look over these words and rank them, with the most neutral word first and the most powerful word last. I'm going to give you sticky notes so you can write one word on each sticky note. Then you can move them around until you have a list your group agrees on."

Jim distributes the sticky notes, and the students get to work. Although Jim moves from group to group, he does not interject himself into the students' conversations because he wants to gauge students' reasoning and depth of understanding of word nuances. When he calls the students back together as a class, he asks, "What was the most difficult part of this task?"

Terri quickly responds, "When we think about something being *plausible*, like in language arts, we think about books, like asking if something could really happen. But not all of these words work in that context, like *fair*, so we had to think about these words in a lot of ways to get a list."

"Okay. Would you bring your group's sticky notes up and put them on the document camera (a machine like an overhead projector but that can project opaque documents, not just transparencies) the same way you have them on your table?"

Terri does. The list is as shown in Figure 7.1.

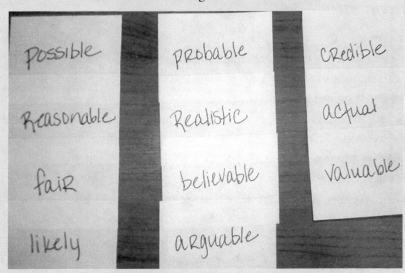

Figure 7.1 *Levels of Meaning*

(Continued)

"I'm curious to know why *reasonable* comes before *fair*. Does anyone have any thoughts on this?" Jim asks.

Marcia offers, "Something may seem reasonable, but that doesn't necessarily make it fair. But I think if something is fair, it also has to be reasonable."

"Do you have an example?"

Marcia thinks for a minute and then continues, "Well, when my older sister turned sixteen, my parents got her a car, but they are telling me they aren't going to get me one. They say that we can share my sister's car and that she can still take me places. I guess this is reasonable because she takes me places now. But it doesn't seem very fair that she got a car and I won't get one."

"But what if your parents got you a car but couldn't afford the insurance for two cars, one for you and one for your sister?" Zach counters. "That may be fair, but it wouldn't be reasonable."

"So do we think this order is correct or incorrect?" Jim asks.

"Even though Zach's got a good point, I think more often than not, if something is fair, in the larger sense of being just, it is also reasonable." Marcia replies.

This type of discussion continues, not so much to create one class list of words on which everyone agrees, but to discuss the relative value of the words in relation to one another.

Differentiation

This activity may prove particularly difficult for English Language Learners. Not only does academic language present a challenge, but cultural differences may overshadow nuances that native speakers will recognize easily. For example, a student from a socialist society may view the notion of fairness as life necessities (medicine, schooling, child care, and so on) as everyone being provided for equally, thus relating *fair* to *equal*. An American student may have a sense that what is *fair* is what is *right* or *just* for the situation.

When working with academic language, you can help English Language Learners by giving them language objectives in addition to content objectives, and by connecting new vocabulary to mastered vocabulary. For example, *residence* is more specific than *house*, but *house* is likely the word that has been mastered. In addition, creating stories around academic words can increase memory through associations.

Picture It

Similar to the Weighty Words activity (Chapter 4) in concept, this strategy challenges students to create a short digital movie to define, conceptualize, and visually present academic words. Easy to create in Apple iMovie or Windows Movie Maker, or even with a video camera, these quick projects help students capture images to remember academic words.

Setup

Break students into small groups and give each group a word to learn and a blank note card. Ask each group to think about how they can visually

---

STEP INTO A CLASSROOM

It is September, and after reviewing some key academic words, Rosaura's eleventh-grade American studies students are making digital movies to demonstrate terminology they will encounter throughout the year. She plans to use the students' movies over the course of the year to keep key academic language fresh in her students' minds.

Wanting to emphasize the planning process instead of focusing on the end result, Rosaura has her students create a storyboard in addition to writing their group's script on a note card.

Reggie, Kirsten, Sari, and Wendy are working with two words: *represent* and *representative*. "What ideas do we have?" Kirsten asks.

"We could do something government-like to show that one person represents a bunch of people," Reggie suggests, wanting to keep the project simple.

"What about doing something more abstract, like having something morph into a symbol that might represent it?" Sari, a future artist, asks.

"Like what?" Kirsten jumps in.

"Well, like we could have a picture of our town turn into a picture of a flag."

"Or a picture of the football team could fade into a picture of our school, showing that our athletes represent our school," Wendy, a cheerleader, says.

"If we do something like that, we could still use Reggie's idea and have a picture of a bunch of people turn into a picture of our state representative. We could get that off his website," Kirsten suggests.

As this idea comes together, Sari begins to sketch out storyboard images. Reggie and Wendy agree to gather the digital images of the town, and Kirsten will gather needed images from the web.

---

communicate their word's definition in a quick video that they will present to the class. They should do more than simply demonstrate the word's denotative meaning, by telling a brief story that shows the word's connotative meaning as well.

For example, the word *reveal* could easily be demonstrated by hiding an object behind a curtain and then moving the curtain to make the object visible, thus revealing the item. But *reveal* has a deeper meaning that goes beyond simply being able to see a thing's outward shape. When something is truly revealed, one gets a sense of its inner characteristics as well.

To make this more apparent, the students might create a brief video story. For example, they could show a few kids passing by a lonely student sitting alone in the cafeteria, and then one student stops, introduces himself, and the two eat lunch together—thus revealing the lonely girl's compassionate nature. The final clip could show a curtain opening to reveal a heart, symbolic of the compassionate boy's inward quality.

Differentiation

If students aren't proficient with Apple iMovie or Windows Movie Maker, or if you don't have the time or the equipment to teach this software, students can use video cameras and act out their stories. Indeed, some words may lend themselves more readily to this type of project anyway.

If students struggle to create their own story, have them find their words in other stories. Although there is merit in having students generate story ideas and take those ideas to fruition, giving them a visual representation of words will help them to remember key vocabulary. To differentiate, ask them to look for examples of these key terms in their everyday life.

A couple of years ago when we adopted our son, we took our daughter out of her first-grade class for two weeks to travel with us when we picked him up. She missed the introduction of shapes in her classroom. Wanting her to continue with school work while we traveled, I asked her teacher for some assignments that she could complete to remain on target with what her class would be studying. We agreed that my daughter could take pictures of various shapes as she encountered them on our trip and write in her journal about where she discovered the various items she photographed. My daughter quickly identified the mirror in our hotel room and the wheels

Julia, a student who enjoys old movies and television shows, is sharing a video clip from *I Love Lucy* with her seventh-grade class. In this particular episode, Lucy is working at a chocolate factory. Her job is to wrap the chocolates as they come down the conveyor belt. Julia explains that her word is *consequence*, which means a conclusion derived from logic.

"I normally think of a consequence as being negative, like in this clip. But really the word has *sequence* in it, so it really means 'what logically comes next.'"

Julia shows the excerpt, in which Lucy, working at the conveyor belt, becomes too confident in her ability. At first she easily keeps up with the pace of the conveyor belt. But as she shows more confidence, the conveyor belt speeds up, and soon Lucy can't wrap the chocolates fast enough. Unwrapped chocolates glide past her. Not wanting to make a mistake, Lucy begins to eat the chocolates she can't wrap. And again, the conveyor belt speeds up. Ultimately, Lucy begins to stuff chocolates anywhere she can. Julia pauses the clip.

"So now Lucy has made several mistakes. Logically, the story only gets funnier if she gets caught, which is one consequence. And then she gets into trouble, which is another consequence." Julia finishes this portion of the episode.

Although Julia did not write the story, she demonstrates a good understanding of *consequence*, an academic word she will encounter across disciplines. Her ability to identify and explain the use of *consequence* in an area of interest shows she is capable of applying the word in novel situations.

To be able to apply words to new experiences, students must understand words and their synonyms. Vocabulary Squares provides a simple puzzle vehicle to encourage kids to play with even the driest of terminology.

on our van as circles. She didn't have to draw a circle to demonstrate understanding. The same can be true with words.

Encourage students to find examples of academic words in action in commercials, television shows, or movies. Ask them to look for examples in magazine ads or articles. Ask students to couple the description (or example, if they can physically bring it in) with a brief explanation of why the found example works, and allow that to demonstrate understanding.

Vocabulary Squares

Using the same templates as they would use for Morpheme Squares (Chapter 2), students create word puzzles using an academic word and a synonym (or antonym). To solve these student-created puzzles, an individual works to find the synonym combinations that will allow all of the small square pieces to form one large square.

Setup

Use a template with either four or nine squares. These can be created by inserting a table into a text document (or using a ruler and pen and paper).

In this example, I have used four squares, thus making the puzzle relatively simple. In this sample, students are using the following sets of antonyms to create their pieces: synonym/antonym, compare/contrast, debate/concur, plagiarize/author, random/sequence.

STEP INTO A CLASSROOM

As students arrive in class, they notice the Do Now written on the chalkboard: "Trade vocabulary squares with a partner and work to solve the puzzle."

Samantha and Bailey, best friends who sit next to each other in their eighth-grade language arts class, trade puzzles. As Mr. Stewart takes attendance, Samantha and Bailey solve each other's puzzles.

"Today we are going to extend our vocabulary squares. For homework, each of you created a four-square puzzle. But for the next few minutes, I would like for you and your partner to create a nine-square puzzle that you will trade with another team." Mr. Stewart distributes a nine-square template, and the students get to work.

As students work, Mr. Stewart notices that Luke and Bill are putting *concur* all of the way around the outer edge of their puzzle. He grins at their shortcut, which creates a border in what is to be a borderless puzzle. "Boys, if you put the same word around the edge, does that really increase the difficulty of the puzzle?"

"Not really," Luke reluctantly agrees. "Can we get another paper?"

When students finish creating and cutting apart their puzzles, Mr. Stewart instructs them to trade with another pair. "As you work in teams to solve your new puzzles, you should tell each other which pieces you need, rather than just moving them around on your desks. So, if you have a piece with *contrast*, you would ask your partner for?"

"*Compare.*"

"I think you have it. Go!"

A buzz fills the room as students work to complete the new task.

---

synonym plagiarize · debate compare	random concur · author synonym
contrast author · concur contrast	antonym debate · random sequence

After students create the puzzles, they cut them apart on the internal lines. Students may then either work to solve their own puzzle or trade with another student. Although the individual sides may pair in a number of ways, only one combination (most likely) will solve the entire puzzle.

In Summary

Although cross-disciplinary academic vocabulary can appear dull on the surface, students must have authentic and meaningful experiences with these words if they are going to take ownership of them and be able to apply their unique meanings in new situations. Yes, these words appear on many standardized assessments, but more important, they give clues to the depth of the task at hand, allowing students to use them effectively throughout their lives.

Discipline-Specific Vocabulary

8

While some words carry their meaning across content areas, many academic words do not. Like a person on vacation, words' personalities can change when they encounter new circumstances. If kids are to be successful, they need to be able to apply the appropriate meaning of multiple-meaning words to the context in which they occur.

In speech communications, for example, the word *expression* might refer to nonverbal cues a person uses to convey meaning—a raised eyebrow to show doubt or disbelief, a head nod to show interest. In mathematics, however, *expression* refers to a mathematical relationship or problem to be solved.

For all students, and particularly for English Language Learners, multiple-meaning words cause problems with understanding. Even a simple word like *bat* can cause a reader to stumble. Is the text about mammals or sports? How can a person *bat an eyelash*? It's all the same word! How are the meanings related? Consider the opening lines of Ernest Thayer's "Casey at the Bat." *The outlook wasn't brilliant for the Mudville nine that day/The score stood four to two with but one inning more to play."* The title of the poem doesn't help us determine the meaning of the word *bat*. The first line gives nothing more to help the reader understand that this poem is about a baseball game. The second line helps only if the reader is familiar with baseball and recognizes the cue words *score* and *inning*.

Perhaps even more confusing than multiple-meaning words, in English we often can use several different words to get across the same meaning, although not all of those words may be the technical terms for the discipline at hand. Again in mathematics, students may use *subtract*, *take away*, or *minus* interchangeably. Initially, this may assist students in understanding that the process of subtraction results in a smaller quantity, but the lack of precise mathematical language could ultimately impede a child's ability to demonstrate complete understanding of the content.

In essence, students must be able to use precise language to communicate, and they must understand that words' meanings can change depending on the situation in which they occur. The following strategies are designed to help students learn about and play with discipline-specific vocabulary.

Multiple-Meaning Maps

Many languages do not use one word to carry multiple meanings. They may instead use several words with more specific meanings where English uses one word to represent many meanings. Remember, for example, the various Greek words for *love* in Chapter 6. English includes thousands of multiple-meaning words, which often confuse non-native speakers. To understand a text, students must first determine the context for multiple-meaning words, and then apply the appropriate context to make meaning while they are reading. As children move through school, multiple-meaning words become more complex, thus requiring even more special attention.

Creating multiple-meaning maps, a well-established idea in the teaching of language, helps students to distinguish between various word meanings and to connect each of those meanings to the appropriate context. Although some would argue that graphic organizers designed specifically for multiple-meaning words are best, a simple web works just as well.

Setup

On the chalkboard (kids can do this individually on a piece of paper while you demonstrate for the class) draw a square for the center of your web. In it, write the multiple-meaning word. From that center, branch out with a line and connected circle for each meaning. In the circles, write a brief definition for each multiple meaning, not the initial word. A map-in-progress for the word *flake* might look like that in Figure 8.1.

After determining each of the word's possible meanings, ask students to draw a picture to help them visualize each definition. If the definition applies to only one discipline, students should also note which discipline that is. After adding drawings and discipline information, the new map looks like that in Figure 8.2.

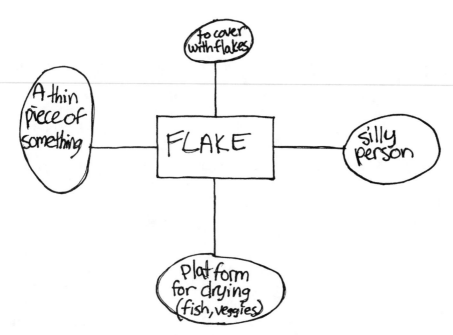

Figure 8.1   *Multiple-Meaning Map*—Flake

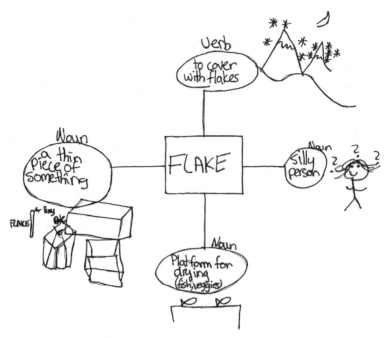

Figure 8.2   *Multiple-Meaning Map*—Flake *(complete)*

As the leaves begin to turn from green to yellow, orange, and red, Marissa's ninth-grade students are beginning their study of mythology, a unit that will take them from the best-known myths of Zeus, Hera, Aphrodite, and Athena, to the great epics of Homer.

Within this study, Marissa wants students to understand that many of the words in English come from Greek, and that many common items we use today are actually named from the Greek gods. From the automobiles we drive (Mercury) to the food we eat (cereal), our ancestors' ideas about the world remain.

Today students will be reading the story of Hercules and Atlas, in which Atlas, who holds up the world, tricks Hercules into taking the burden from him, and how Hercules returns the "favor." But *Atlas* has many meanings, so Marissa and her class create a multiple-meaning map to explore the word further (see Figure 8.3).

Charlie's map shows an understanding of several meanings for the word *Atlas*. In addition to the Titan, Charlie has noted that other meanings include a book of maps, a collection of charts, and so on.

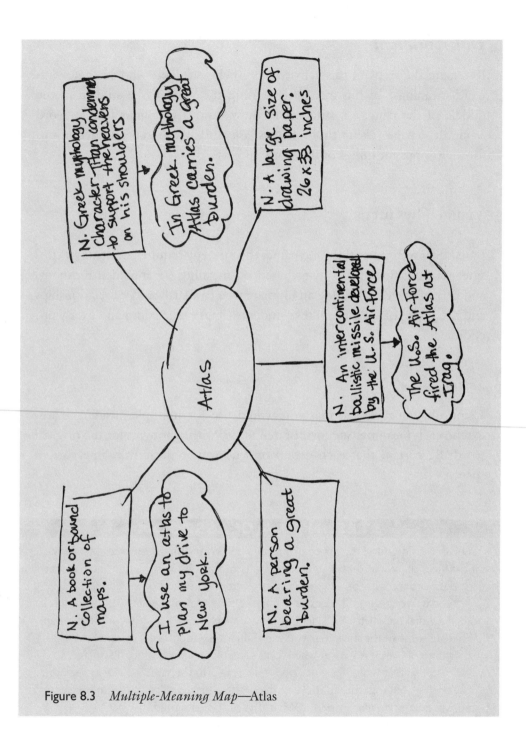

N. Greek mythology character Titan condemned to support the heavens on his shoulders

In Greek mythology, Atlas carries a great burden.

N. A large size of drawing paper. 26 × 33 inches

Atlas

N. An intercontinental ballistic missile developed by the U.S. Air Force

The U.S. Air Force fired the Atlas at Iraq.

N. A book or bound collection of maps.

I use an atlas to plan my drive to New York.

N. A person bearing a great burden.

Figure 8.3   *Multiple-Meaning Map—Atlas*

Differentiation

Reversing the steps of this activity often helps students who struggle with word meanings. In this case, after writing the word to be studied in the middle of the page, ask students to draw various meanings for the word around the page. Using those images, ask students to generate definitions for the various meanings of the word.

Visual Thesaurus

Based on a website of the same name, this strategy requires students to consider relationships of synonyms based on meaning (or intended meaning) and part of speech. Creating an ultimate web to visualize word relationships and categories of meaning allows students to take true command over word choice.

Setup

Using the same web format you would use for multiple-meaning maps, extend each meaning category, or definition, with synonyms for the original word. Be certain that each group of synonyms reflects the same part of speech.

STEP INTO A CLASSROOM

February cold and snow abound outside the classroom windows as Ms. Frasier introduces the visual thesaurus strategy to her tenth-grade students. She has written the word *associate* on the overhead projector and put a box around it.

"Today we are going to extend our multiple-meaning maps into something called a visual thesaurus. We start just like we would with a multiple-meaning map. What are some of the meanings you can think of for the word *associate*?"

James calls out, "A person who works someplace, like an office associate."

"Okay, so that would be a person who engages in the same activity as someone else, or they join together to do something." She makes a line out from the center and writes *same activity or work*. "What part of speech would that be?"

"Noun," James adds.

"Good. Can you think of any other meanings?"

Lucy, looking a bit confused, says, "I thought the word was *as-so-ci-ATE*, like to know someone and hang out with them."

"Yes, that is an alternate pronunciation. And that is another possible definition." She writes *hang out with* on another extension. "Is it also a different part of speech?"

"Yeah, it's a verb," Lucy adds, looking relieved. The conversation continues in a similar pattern until the class has the web shown in Figure 8.4.

"Great. Now let's think of some synonyms for *associate* that match each of these definitions. What are some other words that mean *hang out with*?"

Kayla, a self-proclaimed royal family expert, says, "Consort, like Prince Albert was the prince-consort, not the king, and Queen Victoria hung out with him and depended on him for advice."

"Interesting thinking. Yes, to *consort* is to hang out with." She writes *consort* on a spoke running out from the appropriate definition. "Others?"

"Affiliate."

Ms. Frasier adds this word onto another spoke radiating out from the appropriate definition. "Are these both verbs, like our definition?"

"Yes."

"Good. Now, in groups, I would like for you to brainstorm additional synonyms to complete the rest of our chart."

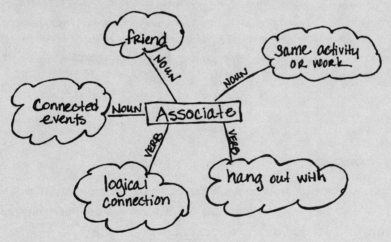

Figure 8.4 *Visual Thesaurus (in progress)*

(Continued)

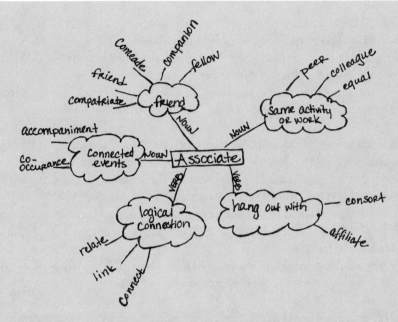

Figure 8.5 *Visual Thesaurus (complete)*

After students have had time to discuss and complete more of the chart, the class compiles their ideas, ultimately creating the web shown in Figure 8.5.

Because words are clustered according to both meaning and part of speech, students will easily be able to see relationships between words. Once this strategy and thought process become natural for kids, they are more apt to select an appropriate alternate word when they write, rather than choosing any word at random when using a regular thesaurus.

Differentiation

The visual thesaurus strategy itself can act as a differentiation tool. The visual nature of the strategy helps kids to picture word relationships, rather than relying on word meanings alone for understanding.

The online visual thesaurus referred to earlier actually allows the user to click on any synonym, which links to lists of all of the synonyms and meanings for that word. If *associate* is the original word, for example, I could click on *consort* and see all of the meanings and synonyms for *consort*, including *associate*. This extension helps kids to better understand the nature and connotative meanings of the synonyms.

Frayer Model

Developed by Frederick Frayer in the late 1960s, the Frayer Model is a concept map for vocabulary. This graphic organizer is divided into four main sections to include the definition, characteristics, examples, and non-examples of words being studied. Revolutionary for its time, this model requires students to both analyze words and apply word knowledge.

Setup

Copy or create a blank Frayer Model. To create one, simply draw a large square and divide the square into four quadrants. In the center, where the quadrants meet, draw a circle. Students will write the word to be analyzed in the circle. (Alternatively, the word can simply be written at the top of the paper, making the circle unnecessary.) Starting in the top-left box and working clockwise, label the boxes *definition, characteristics, examples, non-examples.*

Explain how the chart works to your students. Often students will not understand the importance of non-examples. Although some experts argue that if a student can determine the characteristics and examples of a word, non-examples are insignificant, I believe that defining non-examples helps students to better categorize vocabulary in their minds.

As a class, work though an example using a common word, explaining the new information provided in each box. Using the word *book*, for example, might yield the following definition: *a set of written sheets bound together in a volume.* At this point, one might indeed picture a book, but one might also picture a magazine. Moving to the characteristics box, you might add the following information: *front and back cover, title page, complete work or collection of works, written pages, may include blank pages,* and so on.

To complete the sections for examples and non-examples, students must apply both the word's definition and characteristics to known objects, and then determine whether those objects qualify as examples or as non-examples. In the examples section, students might list *novels, dictionaries, encyclopedias,* and the like. In non-examples, they might include *magazines, newspapers,* and *letters.*

STEP INTO A SCIENCE CLASSROOM

Ms. Anderson's eighth-grade physical science students are studying the concept of *force*. Although the kids have heard and used the word in various settings—a *force* to be reckoned with; she *forced* me to do it—they have yet to master the science-specific definition. After introducing the Frayer Model, she asks students to draw one in their interactive notebooks. Using their notes to guide them, students are working in pairs to complete the chart for the word *force*.

Joanie and Paula are working together. They open their heart and flower-decorated notebooks and begin to look back through their information on *force*. Upon finding the definition, Paula says, "My notes say that force is a push or a pull." The girls write *a push or a pull* in the *definition* box.

"I have something here about force being measured in newtons," Joanie adds.

"I guess that would be a characteristic, right?" Paula asks.

"Yeah. It's not the definition, and it isn't an example, so it must be a characteristic." The girls write this information in their chart and then continue looking through their notes.

Joanie adds, "And here's something about force being able to move objects and change their speed."

"And force can stop something from moving, too," Paula says. "Remember when we threw the ball in class and when someone caught it, Ms. Anderson explained that the force of the person's hand made the ball stop."

Figure 8.6 shows what the girls' charts look like at this point.

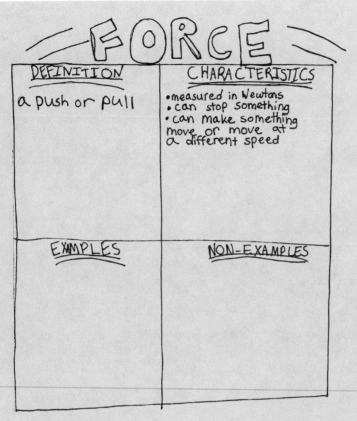

Figure 8.6 *Frayer Model Map—Force #1*

"Okay," Joanie says, "what do we have for examples and non-examples?"

"I don't have anything in my notes about that."

"I think that's because we have to come up with those now," Joanie sighs. "Let's see if we can find things in our notes that would not be examples of force."

"Well, *acceleration* isn't the same as *force*. Acceleration is the change in velocity over time. It can be impacted by force, like the force of gravity, but it isn't an example of force."

"Oooo, that's so good!" Paula agrees. They write *acceleration* under *non-examples*. "That would mean that *speed*, *velocity*, *mass*, *weight*, *power*, and *work* aren't examples of force either!" They add these terms to their chart.

(Continued)

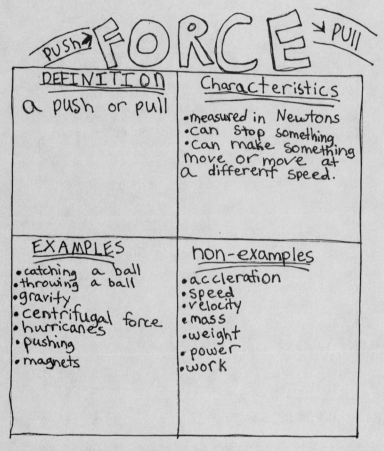

Figure 8.7 *Frayer Model Map—Force #2*

"Okay, so what *are* examples of force?" Paula asks.

"What about a person catching a ball, like you said earlier?"

"I think that's one. And throwing the ball is an example of force, too." The girls continue adding examples until their chart looks like what's shown in Figure 8.7.

After students have had time to work in pairs, Ms. Anderson pulls the class together for discussion. During this time, she not only checks their understanding of force, but also uses the discussion as an opportunity to review other key terminology like *acceleration*, *velocity*, *speed*, and so forth.

As the new school year begins, Ms. Bishop is introducing the morpheme *bio* (life) to her sixth-grade students. As the students generate a list of words they already know using this morpheme, Becky, a petite girl with glasses, asks, "What's the difference between *biography* and *autobiography*?"

"Does anyone know the answer?" Ms. Bishop questions.

"Well, they are both stories about a person's life," Philip says grinning, exposing his dimples.

"Yes. That's true. And that relates to our morpheme *bio*. But what is the difference between the two?" Ms. Bishop questions again.

"I think an autobiography is something you write about yourself." Daisy responds.

"Good. And a biography?"

"I guess it's something you write about another person," Daisy continues.

"Yes. So because I still sense some hesitation, let's do another activity with the word *biography*. In this activity, we are going to fill in four squares of information about the word *biography*." She draws a Frayer Model on the chalkboard and asks the students to copy it onto their papers. "Based on our discussion, what do we think might be the definition of *biography*?"

Daisy repeats, "A story a person writes about someone else."

As Ms. Bishop models, the students write the definition in the first box. Ms. Bishop continues, "Okay, so what are some characteristics of a biography?"

Inez says, "Well, if someone writes about my life, I hope he tells the truth."

"Okay, so that's what type of writing—fiction or nonfiction?"

"Nonfiction," Inez, bright-eyed and smiling, responds.

"Anything else?" Ms. Bishop prompts.

Antonio says, "It would probably start at the beginning of the person's life and go to the end of it, like in order."

"That's chronological order," Ms. Bishop clarifies. The students continue to fill in their papers. Figure 8.8 shows what Claudia's paper looks like at this point in the lesson.

"Great. So our charts now have the definition and characteristics. Sometimes, though, it's helpful to have some examples and non-examples, meaning things that aren't good matches, to help us identify what something is, or isn't. In the non-examples box, it's important to list things that might likely be confused with the word we are studying, in this case, *biography*. We don't want to be silly and list all of the things a biography is not, like a chair. We all know that. So when you are working on this section, you want to think about types of writing that would not be an example of a biography.

(Continued)

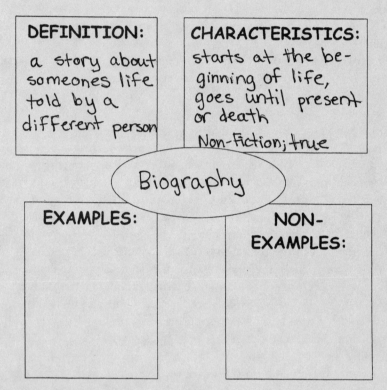

The Frayer Model Map
On __Biography__

DEFINITION:
a story about
someones life
told by a
different person

CHARACTERISTICS:
starts at the be-
ginning of life,
goes until present
or death
Non-Fiction; true

Biography

EXAMPLES:

NON-
EXAMPLES:

Figure 8.8 *Frayer Model Map*—Biography #1

"Let's look at our papers—you see that you have spaces for both examples and non-examples. Working with a partner, please talk about and complete these two boxes."

As students work, Ms. Bishop moves around the room to answer questions as they arise and to check on students' progress. After a few minutes of working with Anya, Claudia's paper has progressed to look like Figure 8.9.

Through this process, Claudia has been able to denote that a biography may, indeed, take many forms, not just the typical book one might initially consider. Because of this process, she will be better able to distinguish biographies and biographical information when she encounters it.

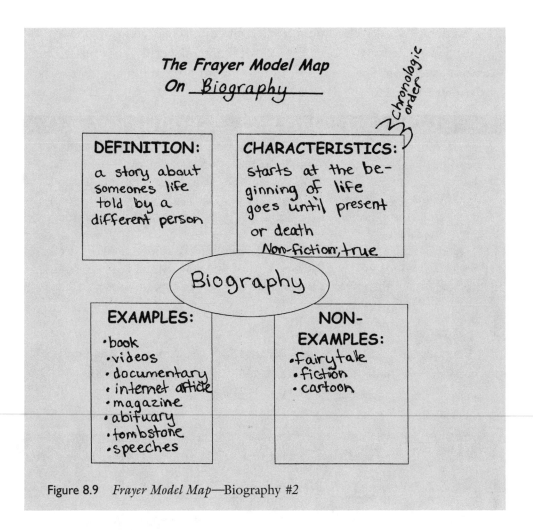

The Frayer Model Map
On __Biography__

Chronologic order

DEFINITION:
a story about someone's life told by a different person

CHARACTERISTICS:
starts at the beginning of life goes until present or death
Non-fiction, true

Biography

EXAMPLES:
- book
- videos
- documentary
- internet article
- magazine
- abituary
- tombstone
- speeches

NON-EXAMPLES:
- fairytale
- fiction
- cartoon

Figure 8.9   *Frayer Model Map*—Biography #2

Academic Word Walls

Like Morpheme Walls (Chapter 2), Academic Word Walls display the vocabulary that students need to master and be able to access as they learn new content. As previously stated, word walls displaying random collections of words are better than no word walls at all, but word walls designed for specific purposes and sets of vocabulary help clarify and enrich students' understanding.

Academic Word Walls should be fluid and interactive, allowing opportunities for students to sort and re-sort content-specific vocabulary. In essence, they combine the best features of word walls and of concept sorts (Chapter 5).

STEP INTO A CLASSROOM

As part of their review for the mid-year exam, Ms. Laurie's ninth-grade students are working in groups to sort and re-sort their academic vocabulary. Because her classroom is divided into stations (including a Morpheme Wall, an Academic Word Wall, a writing center, a publishing station, a classroom library, and a computer station), she has divided the students into small groups that will rotate among the stations.

Alonzo, Kayla, Lucy, and Jose are working to sort the words on the Academic Word Wall into the following categories, based on the header card Ms. Laurie has provided them with: *figurative language, story, drama, poetry,* and *research*. Here is the result of their sort:

Figurative Language	Story	Drama	Poetry	Research
metaphor	protagonist	lighting	ballad	database
simile	antagonist	set design	epic	search engine
personification	setting	blocking	sonnet	plagiarism
symbolism	tone	makeup	lyric	citation
allusion	point of view	costume	ode	paraphrase
imagery	theme	voice	simile	quotation
oxymoron	narrator	expression	metaphor	
	dialogue	cues	personification	
	foreshadowing	monologue	imagery	
	flashback	soliloquy	symbolism	
	characterization	dialogue		
	irony	aside		
	hyperbole	comedy		
	pun	tragedy		
	dialect			
	stereotype			
	caricature			

After they have completed the first sort, Ms. Laurie hands the students another set of header cards and asks the students to re-sort the words. Their new sort looks like this:

Literary Technique	Tools	Form
metaphor	costume	comedy
simile	blocking	tragedy
personification	lighting	epic
rhetorical question	set design	ballad
allegory	database	sonnet
allusion	search engine	lyric
imagery	makeup	ode
oxymoron		
foreshadowing		
irony		
hyperbole		
pun		
dialect		
stereotype		
caricature		
dialogue		
aside		
soliloquy		

Setup

Begin building your Academic Word Wall with those words students will encounter throughout the term. Put these words on note cards, and place them on the wall. Because you and your students will be physically moving words to sort them, you may wish to laminate index cards with all of the key vocabulary for the term before creating the wall. If your room has a carpeted room-divider (or a carpeted wall), you can put Velcro on the back of cards to make them easier to move around. Alternatively, if your chalkboard is magnetic, you can purchase a strip of cheap magnets at a craft store to achieve the same effect. Personally, I use the free magnets that come on pizza boxes and in the mail as advertisements and use double-stick tape to attach them to my word cards.

Throughout the term, add new vocabulary to the wall as it is taught. With each new collection of words added, you can encourage students to work in small groups to sort and re-sort the words by various characteristics.

Differentiation

Not all of the words on the wall need to be in play all of the time. Limiting the number of words and categories will assist those students who feel overwhelmed as the word wall grows.

Parody Poems/Raps

Ultimately, students should be able to produce, not simply to receive, academic language. But academic language can feel dry and dull, which is all the more reason to find playful ways to help students engage with these new words. Like singing the prepositions to the tune of "I'm a Yankee Doodle Dandy" or memorizing the names of the bones to the tune of "Ham-bone," this strategy challenges students to make academic words more fun—which also helps them more readily retain the new words they are learning.

Setup

Find examples of song parodies to share with your students. Personally, I like many of the songs by The Capitol Steps, a comedy group that jabs at political figures and social situations. Explain to students that parodies are familiar songs with rewritten lyrics. Although students may not be familiar with the term *parody*, they generally know the concept and can give back additional examples.

It is the first week of school and, while summer still lingers in the air, Karen's eighth-grade students are adapting to the new schedule of school. She wants to learn more about their critical thinking skills, so Karen asks students to write parodies about the adjustment to eighth grade—both being back in the routine of school and the expectations for work. Although students are allowed to work in groups, Katherine opts to work individually and begins to tap out the beat to her favorite Lonestar song with her pencil. As the rhythm of the music moves in her head, Katherine writes the parody. Katherine's parody works in rhyme so as she thought through the topic she considered many possible word choices and sentence variations to mimic the rhyme of the original song.

After breaking students into groups, explain that each group will write a parody of a school-appropriate song of their choice in which they will be expected to use and define some of the academic language they are learning in class. Then set out the criteria you believe is appropriate for your students: number of stanzas, words to be used, performance standards, and the like.

Differentiation

The very act of plugging information into song or rhyme form helps students to memorize necessary information. Think about the last time you heard "Hickory Dickory Dock." Unless you spend lots of time around young children, it's probably been a while, and yet you can probably recite the second line without much thought: "The mouse ran up the clock." Patterns help us learn and retain information.

Writing parodies challenges students to work within an established structure (the structure of the song they've chosen) while demonstrating understanding of new terminology. For some students, starting with a blank slate may be easier than conforming to an existing song's format. Allowing students to write raps also often proves less daunting, as they can beat-box around words, creating their own structure.

In Summary

Academic vocabulary, although necessary for understanding various disciplines, often seems dry and uninteresting, and can present significant obstacles for students. Because discipline-specific words rely on context for clear meaning, students need to be taught strategies that will help them to learn about the various contexts in which words might appear, and to apply words in appropriate ways. Giving these academic words a place of significance in instruction helps students to *learn* them; using strategies that make these words fun to learn helps students to *retain* them.

Closing Thoughts

When I read a text, I often wonder how the writing of the text has changed the author. Of course, before writing a book myself, I made sweeping assumptions about this, but now I know it to be true—writing a book changes you.

When I first contemplated this text, I was fraught with worry that my experiences with learning and teaching language wouldn't lend any insight to readers. But writing this book has helped me to see not only what I know about language and the teaching of language but how much more there is to learn.

Yes, I have shared strategies that engage even the most reluctant learners, helping them to see that this thing we call language is a truly unique and awesome invention. For us, it is the way we both learn about and express our ideas about the world in which we live. It is our most reliable vehicle for sharing our thoughts and having them be clearly understood.

Even more fascinating is that we use and learn language simultaneously. Texts that cause us to consider context and multiple meanings stretch our understanding of words. Idioms and regional dialects both confuse and enlighten us—and sometimes provide a little amusement to boot. After all, who isn't enchanted by a Southerner's or Irishman's lilt?

The very dynamic nature of language ensures that it will forever be a field of interest and of scholarly study as words morph into new words or meanings, as new words are added, and as other words become obsolete.

Recently I saw a picture of the first typewriter. Typewriters exist today in museums, a few offices, and, admittedly, in my closet. Keyboards, not the piano-type—for that's another story—have replaced typewriters and have caused the addition of new words and uses in our language. What will be next? Perhaps one of our students will invent the language to accompany the latest technological advances.

This text also required me to dig back through many years of study, attend workshops, work with true experts in linguistics, and synthesize what I have learned. And honestly, when I tried some of these strategies for the first time in my own classroom, it was out of desperation, a brainstorm, or a sense that it certainly couldn't hurt. Sharing them in this format challenged me both to reflect on the value of each strategy and to articulate it in a way I never have before.

Most important, writing this text has caused me to do what it encourages for students—to play with words. After my initial grappling to find the right words, my editors and I have toyed with dozens of other possibilities. Each option presented a new connotation, a new way of thinking about the meaning I wanted to convey. At times I just wanted to get something down on paper, but always, always I came back to the play and the sheer joy (and often relief) of finding just the right word.

Appendix A

Morpheme Square Templates

Appendix A.1 *Morpheme Squares—4 Boxes*

May be copied for classroom use. © 2008 by Sandra R. Whitaker, from *Word Play* (Heinemann: Portsmouth, NH).

<table>
<tr><td></td><td></td></tr>
<tr><td></td><td></td></tr>
<tr><td></td><td></td></tr>
</table>

Appendix A.2 *Morpheme Squares—6 Boxes*

May be copied for classroom use. © 2008 by Sandra R. Whitaker, from *Word Play* (Heinemann: Portsmouth, NH).

Appendix A.3 *Morpheme Squares—9 Boxes*

May be copied for classroom use. © 2008 by Sandra R. Whitaker, from *Word Play* (Heinemann: Portsmouth, NH).

Appendix B

Wordsters Letter Combinations

ABL	BEL	CRE	GIT
ABS	BET	CRO	GLA
ACC	BGR	DAP	GRA
ACE	BIO	DEN	GRE
ACT	BLY	DIP	HAI
AFT	BON	DIS	HAT
AGE	BRE	DUP	HER
AIN	CAM	EAR	HIG
AIR	CAT	ENE	ICK
ALT	CET	ETE	ING
AME	CHA	EVE	INN
ANT	CHE	EXI	INT
APT	CIT	FAN	ION
ARC	CLE	FIN	IVE
ARG	CLO	FIS	JIP
ASL	COM	FIT	JOV
BAT	CON	FOO	KNO
BBL	COR	FUR	KRS

LAB	NES	PUR	STL
LAN	NET	QUA	STU
LAW	NOR	QUE	SYN
LES	NTH	QUI	TAB
LIF	OPT	RAC	TBL
LFT	OSS	RAI	TCE
LLE	OTH	REA	TEA
LMP	OUT	REC	THE
LOT	OVE	REP	TIP
LPE	PAN	RES	TRA
LRN	PBL	RLE	TRE
MAE	PCE	ROA	TTE
MAP	PEN	SAC	TWL
MEL	PHY	SAT	UNL
MER	PIN	SCR	VAL
MES	PIO	SER	VOC
MIO	PLE	SET	VOW
MIT	POS	SHE	VOY
MLE	POT	SKT	WEL
MME	PRE	SLE	WHE
MST	PRO	SNO	WHI
NAL	PRW	SPA	YEN
NAU	PSY	SSI	YET
NBL	PUD	STA	ZED

Appendix C

Weighty Word List

Alibi
Approximate
Aptitude
Arbitrary
Artifact
Assimilate
Asterisk
Bassinet
Bogus
Camouflage
Caravan
Carnivorous
Catadromous
Document
Dominator
Draconian
Duplicate
Elevation
Elocution
Epigram
Extraneous

Fantasy
Fatuous
Filibuster
Fragmented
Gallantry
Genuine
Gerrymander
Gramophone
Harlequin
Herculean
Hijack
Hospitality
Identity
Impertinent
Infinitesimal
Insipid
Intrepid
Itinerary
Jargon
Jettison
Juvenescent

Kaleidoscope
Kleptomania
Laborious
Lassitude
Leadership
Malleable
Meander
Miasma
Miscellaneous
Monopoly
Monotonous
Neophyte
Notarize
Obligated
Operate
Optimum
Ostentatious
Paradise
Paramount
Predominate
Pseudonym

Publication	Simultaneous	Victorious
Quantify	Solitude	Wainwright
Quarantine	Superfluous	Whimsical
Quotable	Territory	Willy-Nilly
Rambunctious	Timorous	Wisecrack
Reciprocate	Transparent	Xenon
Reclusive	Ultimatum	Xiphoid
Recognize	Utility	Yeoman
Replicate	Vernacular	Zealous
Sanctify	Veteran	Zeppelin
Secondary	Vicarious	Zoology
Serendipity	Victory	

Appendix D

References

Allen, Janet. 1999. *Words, Words, Words: Teaching Vocabulary in Grades 4–12.* York, ME: Stenhouse.

Allington, Richard L. 2001. *What Really Matters for Struggling Readers: Designing Research-based Programs.* New York: Addison Wesley Longman.

American Heritage Dictionary editors. 1995. *Roget's II The New Thesaurus, 3rd ed.* New York: Houghton Mifflin Company.

Anderson, Richard, and William Nagy. 1992. "The Vocabulary Conundrum." *American Educator* (Winter): 14–18, 44–47.

Baumann, James F., and Edward J. Kame'enui, eds. 2004. *Vocabulary Instruction: Research to Practice.* New York: The Guilford Press.

Bear, Donald R., Marcia Invernizzi, Shane R. Templeton, and Francine Johnston. 1999. *Words Their Way: Word Study for Phonics, Vocabulary, and Spelling Instruction.* New York: Pearson Education.

Beck, Isabel L., Margaret G. McKeown, and Linda Kucan. 2002. *Bringing Words to Life: Robust Vocabulary Instruction.* New York: Guilford Press.

Beers, Kylene. 2003. *When Kids Can't Read: What Teachers Can Do.* Portsmouth, NH: Heinemann.

Biemiller, Andrew. 1999. "Language and Reading Success." In *From Reading Research to Practice, A Series for Teachers*, edited by Jeanne Chall. Cambridge, MA: Brookline Books.

———. 2001. "Teaching Vocabulary: Early, Direct, and Sequential." *American Educator* 25 (Spring): 24–29.

Bromley, Karen. 2007. "Nine Things Every Teacher Should Know About Words and Vocabulary Instruction." *Journal of Adolescent and Adult Literacy.* Newark: International Reading Association.

Carroll, Lewis. 1946. *Alice's Adventures in Wonderland and Through the Looking Glass.* New York: Penguin Young Readers Group.

Costello, Robert B., ed. 2000. *The American Heritage Dictionary, 3rd ed*. New York: Houghton Mifflin Company.

Cunningham, Anne. 2004. LETRS Training. Monterey, CA.

Cunningham, A., and K. Stanovich. 2003. "Reading Can Make You Smarter." *Principal*, 83 (November/December): 34–39.

Ebbers, Susan M. 2004. *Vocabulary Through Morphemes: Suffixes, Prefixes, and Roots for the Intermediate Grades*. Longmont, CO: Sopris West Educational Services.

Estes, Tom, and Rolin D. Larrick. 2007. *Word Build*. Keswick, VA: Dynamic Literacy.

Flavell, Linda, and Roger H. Flavell. 1995. *Dictionary of Word Origins*. London: Kyle Cathie Limited.

Frasier, Debra. 2000. *Miss Alaineus: A Vocabulary Disaster*. New York: Harcourt.

Frayer, D., W. C. Frederick, and H. J. Klausmeier. 1969. *A Schema for Testing the Level of Cognitive Mastery*. Madison, WI: Wisconsin Center for Education Research.

Freeman, David E., and Yvonne S. Freeman. 2004. *Essential Linguistics: What You Need to Know to Teach Reading, ESL, Spelling, Phonics, Grammar*. Portsmouth, NH: Heinemann.

Ganske, Kathy. 2000. *Word Journeys: Assessment-guided Phonics, Spelling, and Vocabulary Instruction*. New York: Guilford Press.

Gies, Miep, and Alison L. Gold. 1988. *Anne Frank Remembered*. New York: Simon & Schuster Publishing.

Gove, Philip B., ed. 2002. *Webster's Third New International Dictionary of the English Language Unabridged*. Springfield, MA: Merriam-Webster Inc., Publishers.

Gunter, Mary A., Thomas H. Estes, and Susan L. Mintz. 2006. *Instruction: A Models Approach*. Boston: Allyn & Bacon.

Gwynne, Fred. 1988. *A Chocolate Moose for Dinner*. New York: Alladin.

———. 1988. *The Kind Who Rained*. New York: Alladin.

Harper, Douglas. 2001. *Online Etymology Dictionary*. www.etymonline.com. (accessed April 2007).

Hecht, Jeff. "Oldest Writing in the New World Discovered." *New Scientist*, Sept. 14, 2006. www.newscientist.com/article/dn10076–oldest-writing-in-the-new-world-discovered.html. (accessed June 2007).

Invernizzi, Marcia, Francine Johnston, and Donald R. Bear. 2004. *Words Their Way: Word Sorts for Within Word Pattern Spellers*. Upper Saddle River, NJ: Pearson.

Ivey, Gay, and Douglas Fisher. 2006. *Creating Literacy-rich Schools for Adolescents*. Alexandria, VA: Association for Supervision & Curriculum Development.

Johnson, Dale D. 2001. *Vocabulary in the Elementary and Middle School*. Boston: Allyn & Bacon.

Johnston, Francine, Marcia Invernizzi, and Donald R. Bear. 2003. *Words Their Way: Word Sorts for Letter Name Alphabetic Spellers*. Upper Saddle River, NJ: Pearson.

———. 2005. *Words Their Way: Word Sorts for Derivational Relations Spellers.* Upper Saddle River, NJ: Pearson.

———. 2005. *Words Their Way: Word Sorts for Syllables and Affixes Spellers.* Upper Saddle River, NJ: Pearson.

Karcik, Jeffrey. 2000. *The Word Museum: The Most Remarkable English Words Ever Forgotten.* New York: Touchstone.

Larrick, Rollin D. 2007, May 10. Interview.

"Last female-only language speaker dies." *China Daily*, Sept. 24, 2004. www.china daily.com.cn/english/doc/2004–09/24/content_377436.htm. (accessed June 2007).

Levitt, Paul M., Elissa S. Guralnick, Douglas A. Burger, and Janet Stevens. 2000. *The Weighty Word Book.* Lanham, MD: Rinehart Publishing.

Marzano, Robert J. 2003. *What Works in Schools: Translating Research into Action.* Alexandria, VA: Association for Supervision & Curriculum Development.

Marzano, Robert J., and Debra J. Pickering. 2005. *Building Academic Vocabulary Teacher's Manual.* Alexandria, VA: Association for Supervision & Curriculum Development.

Marzano, Robert J., Debra J. Pickering, and Jane E. Pollock. 2001. *Classroom Instruction That Works: Research-based Strategies for Increasing Student Achievement.* Alexandria, VA: Association for Supervision & Curriculum Development.

Merriam-Webster online. 2007. www.m-w.com. (accessed April 2007).

Michaels, Judith Rowe. 2001. *Dancing with Words: Helping Students Love Language Through Authentic Vocabulary Instruction.* Urbana, IL: National Council of Teachers of English.

Moats, Louisa. 2000. *Speech to Print: Language Essentials for Teachers.* Baltimore, MD: Paul H. Brookes Publishing Company.

———. 2004. *LETRS: Language Essentials for Teachers of Reading and Spelling.* Longmont, CO: Sopris West Educational Services.

Nagy, William. 1988. *Teaching Vocabulary to Improve Reading Comprehension.* Newark, DE: International Reading Association.

Nagy, William E., and Richard C. Anderson. 1984. "How Many Words Are There in Printed English?" *Reading Research Quarterly* 19: 304–30.

Native American Language Net. "Native Languages of the Americas: Preserving and Promoting American Indian Languages." www.native-languages.org (accessed July 12, 2007).

Partridge, Eric. 1983. *Origins: A Short Etymological Dictionary of Modern English.* New York: Outlet Books.

Pinnell, Gay, and Irene Fountas. 1998. *Word Matters: Teaching Phonics and Spelling in the Reading/Writing Classroom.* Portsmouth, NH: Heinemann.

Robinson, Adam. 1993. *Word Smart: Building an Educated Vocabulary.* New York: Princeton Review Publishing.

Simmons, John S., and Lawrence Baines, eds. 1998. *Language Study in Middle School, High School, and Beyond*. Newark: International Reading Association.

Thinkmap, Inc. 2007. *Visual Thesaurus*. www.visualthesaurus.com. (accessed May 2007).

Tomlinson, Carol A. 1999. *The Differentiated Classroom: Responding to the Needs of All Learners*. Alexandria, VA: Association for Supervision & Curriculum Development.

———. 2001. *How to Differentiate Instruction in Mixed-ability Classrooms, 2nd ed*. Alexandria, VA: Association for Supervision & Curriculum Development.

———. 2003. *Fulfilling the Promise of the Differentiated Classroom: Strategies and Tools for Responsive Teaching*. Alexandria, VA: Association for Supervision & Curriculum Development.

Tomlinson, Carol A., and Caroline C. Eidson. 2003. *Differentiation in Practice: A Resource Guide for Differentiating Curriculum*. Alexandria, VA: Association for Supervision & Curriculum Development.

Wood, Katie. 1984. "Probable Passages: A Writing Strategy." *The Reading Teacher*, 37: 496–99.

Wren, Sebastian. "Developing Research-based Resources for the Balanced Reading Teacher: Vocabulary." *BalancedReading.com*. www.balancedreading.com/vocabulary.html. (accessed May 2007).

Works Cited

Beck, Isabel L., Margaret G. McKeown, and Linda Kucan. 2002. *Bringing Words to Life: Robust Vocabulary Instruction*. New York: Guilford Press.

Beers, Kylene. 2003. *When Kids Can't Read: What Teachers Can Do*. Portsmouth, NH: Heinemann.

Biemiller, Andrew. 1999. "Language and Reading Success." In *From Reading Research to Practice, A Series for Teachers*, edited by Jeanne Chall. Cambridge, MA: Brookline Books.

———. 2001. "Teaching Vocabulary: Early, Direct, and Sequential." *American Educator*, 25 (Spring): 24–29.

Carroll, Lewis. 1946. *Alice's Adventures in Wonderland and Through the Looking Glass*. New York: Penguin Young Readers Group.

Cunningham, Anne. 2004. LETRS Training. Monterey, CA.

Cunningham, A., and K. Stanovich. 2003. "Reading Can Make You Smarter." *Principal*, 83 (November/December): 34–39.

Estes, Tom, and Rolin D. Larrick. 2007. *Word Build*. Keswick, VA: Dynamic Literacy.

Frayer, D., W. C. Frederick, H. J. Klausmeier. 1969. *A Schema for Testing the Level of Cognitive Mastery*. Madison, WI: Wisconsin Center for Education Research.

Ganske, Kathy. 2000. *Word Journeys: Assessment-guided Phonics, Spelling, and Vocabulary Instruction*. New York: Guilford Press.

Gies, Miep, and Alison L. Gold. 1988. *Anne Frank Remembered*. New York: Simon & Schuster Publishing.

Gunter, Mary A., Thomas H. Estes, and Susan L. Mintz. 2006. *Instruction: A Models Approach*. Boston: Allyn & Bacon.

Hecht, Jeff. "Oldest Writing in the New World Discovered." *New Scientist*, Sept. 14, 2006. www.newscientist.com/article/dn10076-oldest-writing-in-the-new-world-discovered.html. (accessed June 2007).

Larrick, Rollin D. 2007, May 10. Interview.

"Last female-only language speaker dies." *China Daily*, Sept. 24, 2004. www.china daily.com.cn/english/doc/2004-09/24/content_377436.htm. (accessed June 2007).

Levitt, Paul M., Elissa S. Guralnick, Douglas A. Burger, and Janet Stevens. 2000. *The Weighty Word Book*. Lanham, MD: Rinehart Publishing.

Marzano, Robert J., and Debra J. Pickering. 2005. *Building Academic Vocabulary Teacher's Manual*. Alexandria, VA: Association for Supervision & Curriculum Development.

Milton Bradley. 1991. *Wordsters*. Springfield, MA: Milton Bradley.

Moats, Louisa. 2004. *LETRS: Language Essentials for Teachers of Reading and Spelling*. Longmont, CO: Sopris West Educational Services.

Nagy, W. E., and R. C. Anderson. 1984. "How Many Words are There in Printed English?" *Reading Research Quarterly* 19: 304–30.

Native American Language Net. "Native Languages of the Americas: Preserving and Promoting American Indian languages." www.native-languages.org. (accessed July 12, 2007).

Poe, Edgar A. "The Pit and the Pendulum." http://literature.org/authors/poe-edgar-allan/pit-and-pendulum.html. (accessed May 2007).

Pressman. 1993. *Perpetual Notion*. New York: Pressman Toy Company.

Thinkmap, Inc. 2007. *Visual Thesaurus*. www.visualthesaurus.com. (accessed May 2007).

Wood, Katie. 1984. "Probable Passages: A Writing Strategy." *The Reading Teacher*, 37: 496–99.

Index

Morpheme Walls, 30–36, 159
  classroom use of, 31–34
  differentiation, 34–36
  fluidity of, 34–35
  graffiti component of, 36
  Morpheme Manipulatives and,
    31, 33
  nonsense poems and, 43
  setup for, 30–31, 34
morphemic structure, 15–46
  importance of, 16–18
  Latinate words and, 16–18
  seemingly random *o* and, 20
  student interest in, 46
  student understanding of, 15–16
  teaching, 18
  vocabulary instruction and, 8, 9
  vocabulary strategies and, 20
  word play and, 15
multiple intelligences, 2
multiple-meaning maps, 146–50
  differentiation, 150
  graphic organizers for, 146–49
  setup for, 147
  using, 148
multiple-meaning words, 145–46
multisyllabic words, 78–79, 83
mythology, 148

Nagy, William E, 5, 16, 61, 87
National Spelling Bee, 51
National Treasure, 56
Native American languages,
    49
Native Languages of the Americas,
    49
Newsweek, 121
No Child Left Behind, 131
non-examples, in Frayer Model,
    153, 154, 155, 159

nonfiction
  conceptual sorts in, 106
  Probable Passage for, 96–103
nonsense poems, 43–45
nonsense words
  value of, 48
  word play with, 40
note cards, for word sorts and
    resorts, 38
noun, 133
Noun-Verb-Adverb poems,
    115
novels, conceptual sorts for, 105
Nushu language, 49

o, seemingly random, 20
obsolete words, 49–50
Oliver, Kim, 134
ostentatious, 81
overarching concepts, 88
Oxford English Dictionary, The, 17

parody poems/raps, 162–63
parts of speech
  identifying, in "Jabberwocky,
    The" (Carroll), 42
  morphemes and, 42, 44–46
peasant/paysant, 56
Perpetual Notion, 89–94
  differentiation, 93–94
  setup for, 90–91
  using, 91–92, 93
person markers, 111
philia, 126
phob, 33
phonemes, 19
physical education, conceptual sorts
    in, 106–7
physics, loaded language and, 123
Pickering, Debra, 5, 131

synonyms
    brainstorming, 151–53
    Power of the Incomprehensible
        Essay and, 73–74
syntax, 88–89

technology, vocabulary and, 47
texting, 48
Thayer, Ernest, 145
thesauri
    Power of the Incomprehensible
        Essay and, 72–74
    visual, 150–53
throne, 110, 111
Time magazine, 121
Tomlinson, Carol Ann, xi–xiii, xv
Twist and Flip, 40
typewriters, 166

unbound, 69
"use context" strategy, 5, 6

Velcro cards, for Academic Word
    Walls, 161
visual aids
    for loaded language, 124
    for visual front-loading, 108,
        110
visual front-loading, 108–10
    setup for, 108, 110
    using, 108–9
visual thesaurus, 150–53
    differentiation, 152–53
    setup for, 150
    using, 150–52
vocabulary
    advanced, 70
    basic, 70
    functional, 70
    ownership of, 85

proficient, 70
technology and, 47
vocabulary cards
    for Academic Word Walls,
        161–62
    for Perpetual Notion, 90–93
vocabulary development
    language-rich environments and,
        4–5
    Matthew Effect and, 9
    reading comprehension and, 5
    reading fluency and, 5
    science instruction and, 7–8
    spelling and, 2
vocabulary instruction
    academic instruction and, 3–4
    background knowledge and, 3
    conceptual meaning makers, 8–9
    discipline-specific vocabulary,
        9
    effective, 5
    elements of, 8–9
    embedding into daily work, 3
    explicit, 5
    in middle school, 7
    morphemic structure and, 9
    root words and, 5
    through reading process, 5
    word choice and, 3–4
    words in context and, 3–4
Vocabulary Squares, 141–43
    setup for, 142
    using, 142–43
vocabulary strategies
    focus areas and, 10
    ineffective, 1–2
    morphemic structure, 16–18
    supporting, xiii
    theoretical basis for, 8, 10
    vocabulary word use and, 2

vocabulary words. *See also* words
    choosing, 1–2, 88
    conceptual links among, 89–94
    defining through storytelling,
        78–83
    grouping, 2–3
    student use of, 2
voluntourism, 55

webs
    for visualizing word relationships,
        150–53
    for words with multiple meanings,
        146–49
Weighty Word Book, The (Levitt),
    78–79, 82
Weighty Words, 78–83
    differentiation, 82–83
    graphic organizers for, 78–80
    setup for, 78–79
    using, 79–82
    word list for, 173–74
Whitaker, Sandra, xiii
Who's Your Daddy?, 124–28
    setup for, 127–28
    using, 126–27
Windows Movie Maker, 139, 140
Wood, Katie, 94
word choice
    8-Count and, 66–67, 70–72
    inaccurate, 3–4
word manipulations, 41
word mapping, 126–28
word origins, 52–56
    differentiation, 55–56
    for idioms, 116–17
    setup for, 53–54
word play
    by children, 13
    with idioms, 57–58

morphemic structure and, 15
nonsense words, 40
value of, 166
vocabulary study and, xii
Weighty Word definitions and,
    82
word puzzles
    anagrams, 41
    Morpheme Squares, 26–30
    Vocabulary Squares, 141–43
words. *See also* root words;
        vocabulary words
    Anglo-Saxon, 16–18, 52–53
    in context, 3–4
    creating with affixes, 19–20
    creating with prefixes,
        20
    high-powered, 75–76, 84
    inventing, 15–16, 49
    Latinate, 16–18
    multiple interpretations of,
        126–28
    with multiple meanings, 145–46,
        148
    multisyllabic, 78–79, 83
    new, 47
    nonsense, 40, 48
    obsolete, 49–50
    origins of, 47–48
    ownership of, 85
    SAT vocabulary, 2
word sorts and resorts. *See* sorting
        and resorting
Wordsters, 61–66
    differentiation, 65
    letter combinations, 171–72
    playing, 63, 65–66
    rules of play, 62
    setup for, 62
    using license plate letters, 65